New Models of Inclusive Innovation for Development

T0361092

Inequality and innovation are both rising issues on the international development agenda. Their intersection is inclusive innovation; defined as the inclusion within some aspect of innovation of groups who are currently marginalised. This is a topic of increasing interest and activity. Large firms have been working to deliver innovative goods and services for base-of-the-pyramid consumers: the $c.3$ billion who live on less than US$2 per day. Within poor communities, an influx of new technology, finance and capabilities has spurred more localised innovation.

A variety of different models have been identified by which this activity is organised and implemented, such as inclusive innovation clusters, grassroots innovation, frugal innovation, innovation platforms and inclusive user–producer interactions. This book explores the operation, conceptualisation and impact of these models, and analyses the nature of inclusive innovation practice and research. It will be of interest to researchers, policy-makers, strategists and other practitioners associated with these new forms of innovation.

This book was originally published as a special issue of *Innovation and Development*.

Richard Heeks is Chair in Development Informatics at the University of Manchester, UK. He has been principal investigator for international development research projects funded by DFID, IDRC, UNCTAD, GIZ and other international agencies. He has authored four books and 40 refereed journal articles on various issues of technology and socio-economic development.

Christopher Foster is a Lecturer in the Information School at the University of Sheffield, UK. His research focuses on new technologies and innovation in developing and emerging markets. His recent work has explored the impacts of ICTs on low-income groups in sub-Saharan Africa.

Yanuar Nugroho is a Research Fellow with the Manchester Institute of Innovation Research, University of Manchester, UK and Deputy Chief of Staff for Management and Oversight of Priority Development Programmes at the Executive Office of the President, Government of Indonesia. He has worked and published on a variety of innovation and development issues.

New Models of Inclusive Innovation for Development

Edited by
Richard Heeks, Christopher Foster and Yanuar Nugroho

Routledge
Taylor & Francis Group

LONDON AND NEW YORK

First published 2016 by Routledge

2 Park Square, Milton Park, Abingdon, Oxfordshire OX14 4RN
711 Third Avenue, New York, NY 10017

Routledge is an imprint of the Taylor & Francis Group, an informa business

First issued in paperback 2017

British Library Cataloguing in Publication Data
A catalogue record for this book is available from the British Library

ISBN 13: 978-1-138-94185-4 (hbk)
ISBN 13: 978-1-138-30008-8 (pbk)

Typeset in Times New Roman
by RefineCatch Limited, Bungay, Suffolk

Publisher's Note
The publisher accepts responsibility for any inconsistencies that may have
arisen during the conversion of this book from journal articles to book chapters,
namely the possible inclusion of journal terminology.

Disclaimer
Every effort has been made to contact copyright holders for their permission to
reprint material in this book. The publishers would be grateful to hear from any
copyright holder who is not here acknowledged and will undertake to rectify
any errors or omissions in future editions of this book.

Contents

Citation Information

The chapters in this book were originally published in *Innovation and Development*, volume 4, issue 2 (October 2014). When citing this material, please use the original page numbering for each article, as follows:

Chapter 1
Introduction: New models of inclusive innovation for development
Richard Heeks, Christopher Foster and Yanuar Nugroho
Innovation and Development, volume 4, issue 2 (October 2014) pp. 175–185

Chapter 2
How inclusive can innovation and development be in the twenty-first century?
Theo Papaioannou
Innovation and Development, volume 4, issue 2 (October 2014) pp. 187–202

Chapter 3
Regulating the negative externalities of enterprise cluster innovations: lessons from Vietnam
J.J. Voeten and W.A. Naudé
Innovation and Development, volume 4, issue 2 (October 2014) pp. 203–219

Chapter 4
Nurturing user–producer interaction: inclusive innovation flows in a low-income mobile phone market
Christopher Foster and Richard Heeks
Innovation and Development, volume 4, issue 2 (October 2014) pp. 221–237

Chapter 5
Operationalizing inclusive innovation: lessons from innovation platforms in livestock value chains in India and Mozambique
Kees Swaans, Birgit Boogaard, Ramkumar Bendapudi, Hailemichael Taye, Saskia Hendrickx and Laurens Klerkx
Innovation and Development, volume 4, issue 2 (October 2014) pp. 239–257

Chapter 6
An analysis of power dynamics within innovation platforms for natural resource management
Beth Cullen, Josephine Tucker, Katherine Snyder, Zelalem Lema and Alan Duncan
Innovation and Development, volume 4, issue 2 (October 2014) pp. 259–275

CITATION INFORMATION

Chapter 7
When grassroots innovation movements encounter mainstream institutions: implications for models of inclusive innovation
Mariano Fressoli, Elisa Arond, Dinesh Abrol, Adrian Smith, Adrian Ely and Rafael Dias
Innovation and Development, volume 4, issue 2 (October 2014) pp. 277–292

For any permission-related enquiries please visit:
http://www.tandfonline.com/page/help/permissions

Notes on Contributors

Dinesh Abrol is Professor at the Institute for Studies in Industrial Development, New Delhi, India. He was previously the Principle Scientist for CSIR-NISTADS, New Delhi, India.

Elisa Arond is currently studying for a Ph.D. in the Graduate School of Geography at Clark University, Worcester, MA, USA. She is also a Researcher at the STEPS (Social, Technical and Environmental Pathways to Sustainability) Centre at the University of Sussex, Brighton, UK.

Ramkumar Bendapudi is affiliated with the International Livestock Research Institute in New Delhi, India.

Birgit Boogaard is affliated with the International Livestock Research Institute in Maputo, Mozambique.

Beth Cullen is affiliated with the International Livestock Research Institute in Addis Ababa, Ethiopia.

Rafael Dias is Professor of Applied Sciences in the Grupo de Análise de Políticas de Inovação at the Universidade Estadual de Campinas, Limeira, Brazil. He is the author of *Sessenta anos de política científica e tecnológica no Brazil* (2012).

Alan Duncan is affiliated with the International Livestock Research Institute in Addis Ababa, Ethiopia.

Adrian Ely is Senior Lecturer in the Science Policy Research Unit at the University of Sussex, Brighton, UK. He is also a Senior Lecturer for the Sussex Energy Group. His research expertise is in agro-ecological agriculture, biotechnology, and innovation for sustainability.

Christopher Foster is a Lecturer in the Information School at the University of Sheffield, UK.

Mariano Fressoli is a Researcher at the Instituto de Estudios sobre la Ciencia y la Tecnología, Universidad Nacional de Quilmes, Buenos Aires, Argentina. His research is in the field of the sociology of science and technology.

Richard Heeks is Chair in Development Informatics at the University of Manchester, UK. He has been principal investigator for international development research projects funded by DFID, IDRC, UNCTAD, GIZ and other international agencies.

Saskia Hendrickx is affliated with the International Livestock Research Institute in Maputo, Mozambique.

Laurens Klerkx is a Researcher with the Knowledge, Technology and Innovation Group at Wageningen University, The Netherlands.

Zelalem Lema is affiliated with the International Livestock Research Institute in Addis Ababa, Ethiopia.

W.A. Naudé is a Professor in the School of Management at Maastricht University, The Netherlands.

Yanuar Nugroho is a Research Fellow with the Manchester Institute of Innovation Research, University of Manchester, UK and Deputy Chief of Staff for Management and Oversight of Priority Development Programmes at the Executive Office of the President, Government of Indonesia.

Theo Papaioannou is a Reader in Politics of Innovation and Development at the Open University, UK.

Adrian Smith is Professor of Technology and Society in the Science Policy Research Unit at the University of Sussex, Brighton, UK. He is also a Senior Lecturer for the Sussex Energy Group. His research centres on innovation studies, sustainable development, and the politics of technology.

Katherine Snyder is based at the International Centre for Tropical Agriculture, Nairobi, Kenya.

Kees Swaans is affiliated with the International Livestock Research Institute in Addis Ababa, Ethiopia.

Hailemichael Taye is affiliated with the International Livestock Research Institute in Addis Ababa, Ethiopia.

Josephine Tucker is based at the Overseas Development Institute, London, UK.

J.J. Voeten is a Researcher in the School of Economics and Management at Tilburg University, The Netherlands.

Preface

The chapters of this book are articles that originally appeared in one of the special issues of *Innovation and Development*, an inter-disciplinary international journal from Globelics network, published by Taylor & Francis. http://www.tandf.co.uk/journals/RIAD

Innovation and Development is a relatively young journal born at a particular juncture in the discourse on development. The closing decades of the last century witnessed unprecedented changes in different spheres of economies and societies. This was induced by, among others, technological innovations led mainly by information communication technology and institutional innovations, resulting in increased integration between countries under globalization. In the emerging context of heightened competition, international competitiveness became the only means of survival. With the expanding global production networks and global innovation networks, different sectors across countries got themselves located appropriately in the global value chains. Instances of high rates growth sustained even for decades tended to suggest that achieving faster economic growth is within the reach of the developing world. Unfortunately, however, the episodes of high growth turned out to be not inclusive and sustainable. The challenge, therefore, is to accomplish development that is sustainable and inclusive.

The mandate of *Innovation and Development* has its roots in this new millennium development challenge. Since the role of innovation in development is increasingly being recognized in both the developed and the developing world, an enhancement of our understanding on the interface between innovation and development might help to find ways of addressing many of the developmental issues and making growth process inclusive and sustainable. Hence, understanding the link between innovation, capacity building and development has emerged as a critical issue of concern for academia, practitioners and policy-makers, including international organizations such as the World Bank or United Nations.

But our understanding of the links between innovation and development remains at best rudimentary, notwithstanding an unprecedented increase in studies on development and innovation on the one hand and a heightened interest in development practice on the other. While the two disciplines (development studies and innovation studies) have been growing in parallel, as they are traditionally separated with limited linkages, in recent years there has been an upsurge of interest in innovation issues in development studies. At the same time, with an increasing engagement of civil society organizations in developmental issues, innovative development practices are becoming more visible and their impact felt more than ever before.

By adopting a broader approach to innovation (to include technological, institutional, organizational and others) the journal and this book series aims to provide a forum for discussion of various issues pertaining to innovation, development and their interaction, both in the developed and developing world, for achieving sustainable and inclusive growth.

It is matter of great satisfaction that *Innovation and Development* has been able to lay the strong foundations for integrating innovation studies and development studies through the high quality articles contributed by scholars across the world. These articles dealt with issues pertaining to diverse contexts ranging from primary agriculture to high-end services, and from low technology sectors to high technology sectors operating in both the developing and developed world. In tune with the Globelics research agenda, *Innovation and Development* has also been promoting research and discourse on innovation at the national, regional, sectoral and societal level to facilitate building up systems for learning, innovation and competence building. A unique feature of *Innovation and Development* is its supplementary sections that publish PhD abstracts, web resources for research and innovations in practice.

The editorial board of *Innovation and Development* also takes pride in highlighting the significant contribution of this journal during the last five years of its existence through its special issues that focused on subjects of much relevance for theory and policy. The special issues brought out by the journal dealt with issues that include:

a) Sustainability–oriented innovation systems in China and India, guest editor Tilman Altenburg;
b) Capability building and global innovation networks, guest editors Glenda Kruss and Michael Gastrow;
c) Innovation and global competitiveness: case of India's manufacturing sector, guest editors N. S. Siddharthan and K. Narayanan;
d) Innovation for inclusive development, guest editor Fernando Santiago;
e) New models of inclusive innovation for development, guest editors Richard Heeks, Christopher Foster and Yanuar Nugroho.

We place on record our appreciation for all our guest editors for joining hands with us in our endeavor to take forward the agenda of *Innovation and Development*. We also take this occasion to acknowledge the liberal support that we received from the Editorial Advisory Board and the Scientific Committee. Our special appreciation goes to Taylor & Francis for bringing out this book series from the special issues of *Innovation and Development* and Emily Ross for taking this project to its local conclusion.

It is our hope that this book series will be useful to the academia at large, innovation scholars in particular and the policy-makers concerned.

K. J. Joseph (Editor in Chief),
Cristina Chaminade, Susan Cozzens, Gabriela Dutrénit,
Mammo Muchie, Judith Sutz and Tim Turpin
Editors, *Innovation and Development*

INTRODUCTION

New models of inclusive innovation for development

Richard Heeks[a], Christopher Foster[b] and Yanuar Nugroho[a,c]

[a]Centre for Development Informatics, University of Manchester, Manchester, UK; [b]Oxford Internet Institute, University of Oxford, Oxford, UK; [c]Manchester Institute of Innovation Research, Manchester Business School, University of Manchester, Manchester, UK

This special issue of *Innovation and Development* focuses on inclusive innovation; specifically on analysis of the new models of this form of innovation which are emerging. After discussing the growing need for research into those models, this editorial paper interrogates the meaning of 'inclusive innovation' and what it means to understand inclusive innovation in terms of models. The editorial then outlines the contribution of the papers that make up this special issue before drawing out some lessons for inclusive innovation policy and practice, and discussing future research priorities.

1. Introduction

If the focus of this special issue is on new models of inclusive innovation then, inherently, there must have been some old models that form the basis for comparison. There are two such foundations. First, there is an old model of what, for contrast's sake, we can call 'mainstream innovation'. This is the innovation aimed at middle- and high-income consumers, producing new goods and services that improve the welfare of those consumers and/or producing new processes that improve the productivity of formal producers. By improving the welfare of higher-income consumers but not that of more marginalized consumers, by improving the productivity of formal but not informal producers, and by focusing on economic development rather than social development needs, mainstream innovation was and remains an innovation of inequality (Klochikhin 2012; OECD 2013).

Concerns about these shortcomings of mainstream innovation have led to a search for alternatives. There is nothing new about this, and these older models of inclusive innovation form a second foundation for comparison. One can trace a line from Robert Owen through Lewis Mumford and Mahatma Gandhi to Ernst Schumacher and the debates of the 1970s about appropriate technology; all of which sought to develop alternative models of innovation that would address the needs of those excluded from the fruits of mainstream innovation (Jamison 2006).

But in the past decade or so, there have been a number of changes that can justify the notion that we might identify new models of innovation for development (Heeks et al. 2013):

- significant involvement of the private sector and global value chains in innovation for the poor,
- the development of poor consumers as an accessible mass market,
- growth of technological capabilities within developing countries, and
- the involvement of new technologies especially information and communication technologies such as mobile phones.

These are some of the component parts of a growth in practices that have been given the label 'inclusive innovation' but which have also been given other labels including 'pro-poor innovation', 'below-the-radar innovation', 'grassroots innovation', 'BoP (base-of-the pyramid) innovation', and more (Kaplinsky 2011; Cozzens and Sutz 2012; Ramani, SadreGhazi, and Duysters 2012). Growth in the reality of this alternative or modified form of innovation has been matched by a growth of political and academic interest, driven particularly by both an actuality and a heightened perception of rising inequality. That inequality – as well as being inherently problematic – is also seen as holding back social and economic development in the long run (Stiglitz 2012). Models of innovation have been drawn into this focus on 'inclusive development' (UNDP 2014) or 'shared prosperity' (World Bank 2013a) because, as noted, mainstream innovation is associated with increasing inequality while inclusive innovation is associated with reduced inequality (Cozzens et al. 2007; Lazonick and Mazzucato 2013).

We therefore see growing engagement with inclusive innovation by international organizations such as the World Bank (Goel 2011) and OECD (2013), by national governments such as India (OAPM 2011) and China (World Bank 2012), and by multinationals from global North and South such as Unilever and Tata (Chataway, Hanlin, and Kaplinsky 2014) alongside large- and medium-sized firms. Hand-in-hand with this activity has grown an intellectual engagement with inclusive innovation. Clusters of intellectual activity are reflected in journal special issues – this current issue plus also ones on 'Innovation for Inclusive Growth' (George, McGahan, and Prabhu 2012) and 'Innovation for Inclusive Development' (Santiago 2014). Figure 1 summarizes more general growth in intellectual outputs on the topic.[1]

We can have a reasonable degree of confidence that inclusive innovation will continue to be of importance in future. A content analysis has been undertaken comparing the key texts for the Millennium Development Goals (MDGs) with those for the Post-2015 Development Agenda, in order to pinpoint issues which are rising up or falling down the international development agenda (Heeks 2014). The concept of innovation more than triples its presence within the development discourse from MDGs to post-2015, while inclusivity increases by more than 1000%.

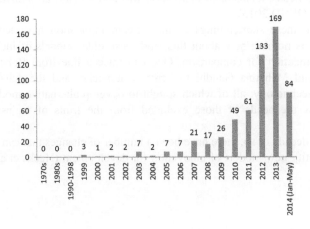

Figure 1.   Growth in intellectual outputs on inclusive innovation.

Their intersection – inclusive innovation – will therefore play an even greater role in development in future than it has done to date.

2. Understanding inclusive innovation

We can divide the content of the literature on inclusive innovation into three categories. Descriptive material just portrays examples of inclusive innovation. Analytical material investigates inclusive innovation through some conceptual lens or framework. Prescriptive material provides guidance on inclusive innovation; running from good implementation practices to arguments about moral framing.

In broad terms, the growth of intellectual output reflected in Figure 1 has been strong on description and on experience-based prescription, but much weaker on analysis and on inquiry-based prescription. Without an analytical foundation, there are concerns that research will not create a critical mass of understanding, and that guidance for innovation policy and practice will be sub-optimal.

Recognition of this analysis gap has prompted a number of initiatives in recent years including the two journal special issues referred to above, one of which emerged from IDRC's short-lived research programme on Innovation for Inclusive Development (IDRC 2011). The analysis gap was also the catalyst for the University of Manchester to organize the July 2013 workshop on 'New Models of Innovation for Development', from which the inclusive innovation-focused papers in this special issue are drawn.

Various elements of inclusive innovation were seen to require further analysis, of which two will be discussed here. First, analysis of the concept of inclusive innovation, covered in this section. Second, analysis of new models of inclusive innovation, covered in the next section of this editorial.

Foster and Heeks (2013, 335) define inclusive innovation simply as 'the inclusion within some aspect of innovation of groups who are currently marginalised'. As Heeks et al. (2013) identify, this cues further discussion about two aspects of the definition in order to more-fully conceptualize inclusive innovation.

The first issue is that of identity: Which groups are seen as historically having been marginalized or excluded, and as needing to be included by new approaches to innovation? Groups identified as the focus for inclusive innovation include women, youth, the disabled, ethnic minorities, and informal sector entrepreneurs (Codagnone 2009; OECD 2013). But the main focus has been the poor: those on lowest incomes, which may typically be defined as less than US$1.25 or US $2.00 or US$2.50 per day.

The second issue is which 'aspect' of innovation the marginalized group is to be included in. The main contrast is between those who think exclusion can be addressed simply in terms of innovation outputs vs. those who think marginalized groups must be included in innovation processes. A more differentiated view is shown in the 'ladder of inclusive innovation' (Figure 2, adapted from Heeks et al. 2013):

- *'Level 1/Intention*: an innovation is inclusive if the intention of that innovation is to address the needs or wants or problems of the excluded group ...
- *Level 2/Consumption*: an innovation is inclusive if it is adopted and used by the excluded group ...
- *Level 3/Impact*: an innovation is inclusive if it has a positive impact on the livelihoods of the excluded group ...
- *Level 4/Process*: an innovation is inclusive if the excluded group is involved in the development of the innovation ...

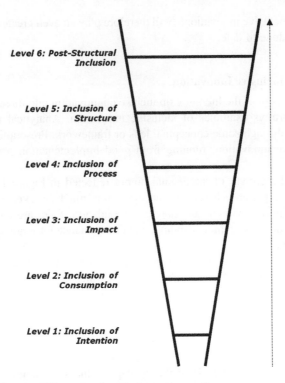

Figure 2.   Understanding the different levels of inclusive innovation.

- *Level 5/Structure*: an innovation is inclusive if it is created within a structure that is itself inclusive ...
- *Level 6/Post-Structure*: an innovation is inclusive if it is created within a frame of knowledge and discourse that is itself inclusive. ...

The levels are akin to steps on a ladder because each level involves a gradual deepening and/or broadening of the extent of inclusion of the excluded group in relation to innovation. In general, each level accepts the inclusion of the levels below, but pushes the extent of inclusion further.' (Heeks et al. 2013, 4–6)

There is no right or wrong 'focus' and 'level', but one needs to recognize within any text on inclusive innovation – be it a policy, public statement, or research paper – which group and which type of inclusion underpins that text. Particular conceptualizations will have particular implications. For example, different marginalized groups will have been subjected to different types of prior exclusion, with different histories and causes (Joseph 2014). Types of inclusion that work for one group will not necessarily work for others creating, for example, the potential for 'illusive inclusion'.

Similarly, the nature of what innovation is understood to be will vary depending on which level of the ladder is accepted as defining inclusive innovation. For the lower levels, innovation will be more of the conventional product/process type. For the higher levels, a broader scope of innovation must be encompassed. The most-recent version of the Oslo Manual (OECD 2005) – arguably the principal global source for defining how we understand and measure the concept of innovation – has moved beyond just product/process to also embrace organizational and marketing changes as innovations. But full acceptance of some concepts of inclusive innovation may require a broader scope still, including quite minor adaptations and appropriations and use variations, and also recognizing that innovation occurs throughout the lifecycle of a new good or service from design through production to diffusion and use (Foster and Heeks 2013). At the highest level of the ladder, innovation may be broadened yet further to include a necessity for change in social structures, social discourse, and frames of knowledge.

3. New models of inclusive innovation

A model is an abstraction from, and a simplification of reality. Its aim may often be to help us understand that reality – which we otherwise could not do because 'true' realities are far too complex for the human mind to encompass – and through understanding, to potentially intervene more effectively.

A variety of new models of inclusive innovation is presented in this special issue, as described further in the next section:

- Innovation platforms (covered in the Swaans et al. and Cullen et al. papers in this special issue) are mechanisms to bring together a group of stakeholders with a focus on innovating to address a particular issue of common interest.
- Cluster innovation (Voeten and Naudé's paper) is innovation that takes place within a co-located group, in which the innovation cannot be attributed to any individual but to a process of group learning. Typically – as in this case – this is a group of micro-/small enterprise owners.
- User–producer interaction (Foster and Heeks' paper) focuses on the learning and innovation which occurs in the connection between producers and consumers.
- Grassroots innovation (papers by Fressoli et al. and Papaioannou) is innovation 'from below', generally associated with innovation emerging from low-income communities.
- Frugal innovation (Papaioannou paper) is innovation that seeks to minimize resource usage, cost and complexity in the production, constitution, and operation of new goods and services.

Models must be recognized as having both pros and cons. If they fulfil the aims stated above, they can make it easier to understand innovation, to communicate and discuss innovation, and to prioritize innovation interventions. But by including only some aspects of reality, they exclude others: while a model throws some elements of innovation into its spotlight, it casts others into shadow.

The very act of giving something a label and calling it a model also has an impact. What does it mean to qualify the word 'innovation' in some way, rather than just calling a phenomenon 'innovation' *tout court*? By giving a new label, do we give a higher profile and priority and more support to the activity? Or do we identify it as being different and liminal? From this, three perspectives on models of inclusive innovation emerged within the July 2013 workshop:

- Inherent Incorporation: the activities of inclusive innovation are already accepted as innovation, and need no additional label. Indeed, labelling may serve to marginalize.
- Deliberate Incorporation: although the activities of inclusive innovation are a form of innovation, they require a new 'innovation *plus*' label in order to justify their acceptance as innovation by some within the field.
- Preclusion: (some of) the activities called inclusive innovation are not actually innovation, and should not be the concern of innovation researchers, policy-makers, or practitioners.

These perspectives are a reminder that models contain the norms and values of those who create them, shaping the thinking of those who use them: what Fressoli et al. refer to as the 'framing' power of models. Examples would include the assumption of innovation platforms that participative approaches to innovation are beneficial or the assumption of grassroots innovation that relatively excluded groups are a source of valuable new ideas. Exposing this framing would require answers to questions such as:

- Who creates this model?
- What is included and what is excluded in the model's abstraction?
- What assumptions does the model make?
- Who benefits from the model?

Alongside these issues of inherent framing, we can also recognize 'framing-in-use': the particular way in which the models are circulated and applied. For example, the extent to which women are or are not included in innovation platforms or the interpreted consumer market for frugal innovations. Again, we could ask questions about who interprets, uses, and promotes particular forms of each model; why they do this; and what impact this has.

One could regress the recognition of framing right up to the very notion of innovation itself but a balance must be struck. Thus, while all six papers in the special issue have an element of critique, three (Voeten and Naudé, Foster and Heeks, and Swaans et al.) restrict this to questioning the operation of each model in practice. But the other three do move further to challenge the models in some way; not just accepting them but unpacking the models and their foundation. Papaioannou reveals the different philosophical underpinnings behind different models of inclusive innovation. Cullen et al. spotlight the power dynamics that shape the formation, interpretation, and implementation of inclusive innovation models. Fressoli et al. expose different ways in which inclusive (specifically grassroots) innovation can be framed, and then track what happens when different framings of inclusive innovation models encounter one another.

4. Contribution of the special issue

As just noted, and unlike the other five papers, Theo Papaioannou's paper – 'How Inclusive Can Innovation and Development be in the 21st Century?' – does not restrict itself to a single model of inclusive innovation. It studies two: frugal innovation and grassroots innovation.

As per the definition above, the core focus of the frugal innovation model is minimization of resource use, cost, and complexity. At best, it might be placed at Level 1 (intention) or just possibly Level 2 (consumption) of the inclusive innovation ladder. First, because marginalized, low-income consumers are not always the target of frugal innovation. The Tata Nano car is an oft-cited example of frugal innovation but – with a minimum price of c. US$2,500 – it is way beyond the means of the more than 3 billion who live on less than US$2.5 per day (World Bank 2013b). Second, because the focus of the frugal innovation model is far more on the process and products of innovation than it is on the consumers and impact of those innovations. Of course, there are multiple interpretations of the frugal innovation model but, for most, any inclusivity would be a by-product rather than an inherent feature.

The grassroots innovation model also focuses on the innovation process but brings the innovator themselves to the fore; that innovator coming from a marginalized group. It therefore sites itself at Level 4 (process) of the inclusive innovation ladder by seeing inclusivity to require the involvement of marginalized group members in early stages of the innovation lifecycle. It places the marginalized innovator at the heart of the process, both exploiting and further enhancing their innovation capabilities.

Papaioannou's paper resonates with the idea of different understandings of inclusivity, as per the ladder model, but it takes its analysis right back to philosophical underpinnings of development. It can particularly be seen to offer new insights into inclusive innovation models from the foundations of development studies, exploring what inclusivity means through lenses of cosmopolitanism, capability theory, and the basic needs approach. Each of these three perspectives presents a different yardstick with which to assess the inclusivity of inclusive innovation models, and Papaioannou argues the potential greater value of the basic needs perspective. His main contribution, therefore, is to remind us that inclusive innovation models are not value-neutral and that it thus behoves those working in this domain to be more explicit about the underlying norms and values which shape their approach to inclusive innovation.

Papaioannou highlights the importance but also current shortcomings of public policy in delivering different visions of inclusive innovation. The paper 'Regulating the Negative Externalities of Enterprise Cluster Innovations: Lessons from Vietnam' by Jaap Voeten and Wim Naudé picks up this theme of policy shortcomings. It does this within the context of the cluster innovation model in Vietnamese craft villages.

We could associate the cluster innovation model with inclusive innovation Level 4 (process) since it focuses on the role of micro-entrepreneurs in innovation, and with Level 5 (structure) since its main interest is the co-located network structure within which the innovation is developed. The strength of this association with Level 4/5 is qualified because there is no necessary connection between innovation clusters and low-income community micro-enterprises. This is more a descriptive model of innovation structure and relations than a prescriptive model of inclusivity, and the cluster could be of much larger firms.

Where applying to micro-enterprises, as in Voeten and Naudé's paper, clusters are often described as involving those on *lower* rather than *lowest* incomes. Many involved, though, are still poor – Sakata (2013) cites average Vietnamese craft village incomes in the 2000s as US $22–66 per month depending on type of craft, compared to average rural farming income of US$17 – and hence it is appropriate to label this as an inclusive innovation model in this instance.

The insights into the cluster model provided by the paper come from an inductive and longitudinal research approach implemented over three years. What this approach found was the negative environmental and social externalities that can materialize from this type of inclusive innovation, and the limited role played by external regulation. The authors find that not just innovation but also an 'internal regulation' of externalities can emerge from inclusive clusters, but in many cases only if facilitated by some degree of external intervention.

The cluster-based view of innovation can be understood as one example of the broader notion of systems of innovation: collections of organizations and institutions which act together to innovate. Traditionally associated only with conventional innovation, systems of innovation are now being identified in relation to inclusive innovation (Foster and Heeks 2013), and this insight underpins the next two papers in the special issue.

Christopher Foster and Richard Heeks' paper 'Nurturing User–Producer Interaction: Inclusive Innovation Flows in a Low-Income Mobile Phone Market' extracts one part from the systems of innovation model – user–producer interaction – which is applied to mobile phone-related innovation in Kenya. Being a model of relations between actors, it has commonalities with the cluster innovation model. It can be associated with Level 4 (process) innovation inclusivity, though it sees intermediaries based in and around low-income communities, rather than end users, as sitting alongside lead-firm producers as innovators. And it could be associated with Level 5 (structure) except that the model represents just one part of a much larger structural whole that would need to be inclusive for this label to properly apply.

Indeed, the main contribution of the paper is to identify two different structural mechanisms for linking producers and users in cases of inclusive innovation: hierarchical vs. market mechanisms. Where the former allows lead firms greater control, it reduces the opportunity for the localized, user-oriented innovations that are vital in diffusing new goods and services to

BoP consumers. Market mechanisms allow greater freedom for such innovation but also for less beneficial innovations, and reduce the potential for 'reverse' flows of learning and innovation from users to producers. Either case, the authors argue, will benefit from enhancing demand-side capability, recognizing the trade-offs between control and freedom for local innovation, and finding ways to reduce the distance between low-income users and innovation producers.

'Operationalising Inclusive Innovation: Lessons from Innovation Platforms in Livestock Value Chains in India and Mozambique' – a paper by Kees Swaans, Birgit Boogaard, Ramkumar Bendapudi, Hailemichael Taye, Saskia Hendrickx, and Laurens Klerkx – continues the systems of innovation theme. It analyses the model of innovation platforms from an inclusive systems of innovation perspective.

The innovation platforms model sits relatively convincingly at inclusive innovation Level 5 (structure). 'Convincingly' because it is a structural model seeking to include the poor – usually farmers since innovation platforms is a model applied largely in agriculture to date – alongside other stakeholders in innovation processes. 'Relatively' because even multi-stakeholder innovation platforms are only sub-structures within the wider structure of national agricultural systems of innovation.

Swaans et al. find that the wider context bled into the functioning of innovation platforms, which they track over a three-year period in India and Mozambique. From this, they identify a set of key issues likely to emerge with innovation platforms – around the nature of actors and their relations, the incentives for innovation, the mechanisms for learning, etc – which then generate some recommendations for practice.

The motif of contextual influences on innovation platforms continues in the next paper: 'An Analysis of Power Dynamics Within Innovation Platforms for Natural Resource Management' by Beth Cullen, Josephine Tucker, Katherine Snyder, Zelalem Lema, and Alan Duncan. In this case, though, rather than deriving insights inductively from practice, the authors derive them deductively through application to innovation platforms in Ethiopia of the 'power cube' framework. Also based around a three-year longitudinal study, three political dimensions are analysed: the shaping of the space within which inclusive innovation takes place; the forms of power – both overt and hidden – which are exercised during inclusive innovation stakeholder selection and interaction, decision-making and implementation; and the different levels of power manifest within inclusive innovation initiatives such as innovation platforms.

Power and its exercise via politics are seen to be central determinants of the outcomes of inclusive innovation models. Inclusive innovation models often challenge existing power structures but, as noted above, those models are typically just sub-structures within a much wider whole. Those wider power structures may continue to dominate, reproducing themselves within the practice of inclusive innovation models and potentially generating innovation without inclusion; at least without Level 5-type (structural) inclusion.

This issue of power is also explored in the final paper of the special issue, 'When Grassroots Innovation Movements Encounter Mainstream Institutions: Implications for Models of Inclusive Innovation' by Mariano Fressoli, Elisa Arond, Dinesh Abrol, Adrian Smith, Adrian Ely, and Rafael Dias. The authors take what can be seen as a Level 6 (post-structural) perspective, understanding the framing of models of inclusive innovation; that is, the way in which meanings and narratives are produced. They then trace these as one particular model – that of grassroots innovation – meets more mainstream innovation institutions in examples from Brazil and India.

These encounters produce two types of results. Grassroots innovation may be inserted into the innovation mainstream but possibly in the form of a scaled, de-contextualized model that betrays some notions of inclusivity. Or grassroots innovation may mobilize and resist, still seeking to provide an alternative to conventional innovation. In either case, the mainstream still dominates innovation discourse and structures. So, at most, a relatively small space for Level 5 or Level 6 inclusion is created. However, Fressoli et al. do demonstrate that inclusive innovation and mainstream innovation are not separate bubbles. They interact and influence each other and the potential is there for mainstream innovation models to become more inclusive. Indeed, the suggestion here is that we should be less concerned with models and more concerned with the process of modelling: the actors and means by which models of inclusive innovation are constructed.

5. Lessons for the future

From any research outputs, one can seek to extract lessons for practice, for policy, and for future research. Individual papers in this special issue have something to say about practice: Voeten and Naudé recommend ways to strengthen local regulation of inclusive innovation; Foster and Heeks recommend ways to improve user–producer interaction; Swaans et al. offer guidance for innovation platform managers, etc. But an overall theme is the way that horizons for good practice expand as one's perspective moves up the inclusive innovation ladder. A Level 3 view on practice will focus simply on improvements to design and use of new goods and services. A Level 4 view will extend this to improve the process by which those innovations are designed, developed, and diffused. A Level 5 view will focus practitioners on recommendations around the structuring of those processes. And the advised starting point from a Level 6 perspective is an examination and understanding of the frames of knowledge which key actors bring to inclusive innovation. We see examples of all these in different papers of the special issue.

Similar lessons can be drawn about policy: alongside the occasional direct recommendation on policy *content*, the papers guide the reader more to consider policy *process* and *structure*. If power structures and framings of inclusive innovation models are central to their ultimate outcomes, the same must also be true of policy for inclusive innovation. Rather than advocating a one-size-fits-all policy menu, the papers presented here thus suggest a more reflective point of departure for policy that seeks first to understand the actors, perspectives, and politics of inclusive innovation.

Lessons for future research can begin with the disciplinary map shown in Figure 3. This argues that, in simple terms, inclusive innovation can be understood as the intersection of innovation studies (IS) and development studies, with each of those fed by broader cognate disciplines.

We can interpret this map in two ways. It is a guide to sources of conceptual frameworks that can inform the study of inclusive innovation models. And it is a guide to the intellectual audiences for research on inclusive innovation models. Inclusive innovation research has been fairly good at engaging with IS; for example, making use of IS frameworks such as systems of innovation (as do the papers by Foster and Heeks, and Swaans et al.) and ensuring a presence at fora such as the Globelics annual conferences.

To date, inclusive innovation research has been less good at engagement with development studies, but this special issue provides some pointers. Papaioannou's paper shows directly and foundationally how this can happen, and other papers offer possible routes by speaking a language that development studies audiences would understand: of externalities and regulation (Voeten and Naudé), of power and politics (Cullen et al.), and of framing (Fressoli et al.). The importance of this engagement must be stressed. As previously explained, inclusive innovation will have a presence in the Post-2015 Development Agenda, and development-based policy and practice audiences will look to research for guidance.

We already have some sense of priority guidance topics from a research demand study that surveyed a policy and practice audience, as summarized in Table 1 from three perspectives (Heeks et al. 2013).

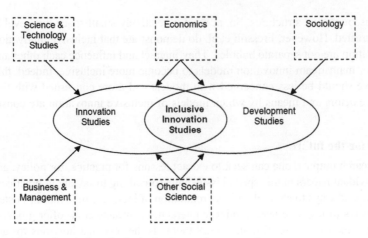

Figure 3.   Disciplinary foundations for inclusive innovation research.

Table 1.   Summary of inclusive innovation research priorities.

Perspective	Research priority
Stakeholder	Policy for inclusive innovation
	Grassroots innovation
	Inclusive innovation intermediaries
Systemic	Basics of inclusive innovation
	New models of inclusive innovation
	Informatics and inclusive innovation
	Benchmarks for inclusive innovation
Process	Readiness for inclusive innovation
	Inclusive innovation good practice
	Scaling inclusive innovations
	Impact evaluation of inclusive innovation

The papers presented in this special issue have provided new insights into a number of these topic areas, not least of course 'New Models of Inclusive Innovation'. The challenge ahead will be building a programme of research sufficient to generate a critical mass of new evidence and ideas for each one of these inclusive innovation research priorities. But policy and practice must not be the only guides for such a research programme. In the academic tradition, future research must also 'speak truth to power' and interrogate further the framing and politics of inclusive innovation models.

Acknowledgements

The 'New Models of Innovation for Development' workshop from which papers for this special issue were selected was financially supported by the Institute for Development Policy and Management, and the Manchester Institute of Innovation Research; both of the University of Manchester, UK. The workshop was supported by the UK Development Studies Association. The editors also wish to thank the attendees and rapporteurs of the workshop, and the anonymous reviewers for the papers in this special issue. Each of the papers went through two rounds of review and revision, a first round of non-blind rapporteur and workshop organizer comments at the time of the workshop, and then a second round of double-blind review by two referees as part of the special issue process.

Note

1. Publication date data from Google Scholar search term 'inclusive innovation' excluding patents and citations.

References

Chataway, J., R. Hanlin, and R. Kaplinsky. 2014. "Inclusive Innovation: An Architecture for Policy Development." *Innovation and Development* 4 (1): 33–54.

Codagnone, C. ed. 2009. *Vienna Study on Inclusive Innovation for Growth and Cohesion*. Brussels: European Commission.

Cozzens, S., E. Kallerud, L. Ackers, B. Gill, J. Harper, T. S. Pereira, and N. Zarb-Adami. 2007. Problems of Inequality in Science, Technology, and Innovation Policy, Working Paper 5, James Martin Institute, University of Oxford, UK.

Cozzens, S., and J. Sutz. 2012. *Innovation in Informal Settings: A Research Agenda*. Ottawa: IDRC.

Foster, C., and R. Heeks. 2013. "Conceptualising Inclusive Innovation: Modifying Systems of Innovation Frameworks to Understand Diffusion of New Technology to Low-Income Consumers." *European Journal of Development Research* 25 (3): 333–355.

George, G., A. M. McGahan, and J. Prabhu. 2012. "Innovation for Inclusive Growth: Towards a Theoretical Framework and Research Agenda." *Journal of Management Studies* 49 (4): 661–683.

Goel, V. K. 2011. "Instruments to Promote Inclusive Innovation." Paper presented at Inclusive Innovation Workshop, Bangkok, March 4.

Heeks, R. 2014. From the MDGs to the Post-2015 Agenda: Analysing Changing Development Priorities, IDPM Development Informatics Working Paper no.56, University of Manchester, UK.

Heeks, R., M. Amalia, R. Kintu, and N. Shah. 2013. Inclusive Innovation: Definition, Conceptualisation and Future Research Priorities, IDPM Development Informatics Working Paper no.53, University of Manchester, UK.

IDRC. 2011. *Innovation for Inclusive Development*. Ottawa: IDRC.

Jamison, A. 2006. "Social Movements and Science." *Science as Culture* 15 (1): 45–59.

Joseph, K. J. 2014. "Exploring Exclusion in Innovation Systems." *Innovation and Development* 4 (1): 73–90.

Kaplinsky, R. 2011. "Schumacher Meets Schumpeter: Appropriate Technology Below the Radar." *Research Policy* 40 (2): 193–203.

Klochikhin, E. 2012. "Linking Development and Innovation: What does Technological Change bring to the Society?" *European Journal of Development Research* 24 (1): 41–55.

Lazonick, W., and M. Mazzucato. 2013. "The Risk-Reward Nexus in the Innovation–Inequality Relationship." *Industrial and Corporate Change* 22 (4): 1093–1128.

OAPM. 2011. Towards a More Inclusive and Innovative India. Office of the Advisor to the Prime Minister, Government of India, New Delhi.

OECD. 2005. *Oslo Manual: Guidelines for Collecting and Interpreting Innovation Data*. Paris: OECD.

OECD. 2013. *Innovation and Inclusive Development*. Paris: OECD. http://www.oecd.org/sti/inno/oecd-inclusive-innovation.pdf

Ramani, S. V., S. SadreGhazi, and G. Duysters. 2012. "On the Diffusion of Toilets as Bottom of the Pyramid Innovation." *Technological Forecasting and Social Change* 79 (4): 676–687.

Sakata, S. 2013. "Rural Industries in Northern Vietnam." In: *Vietnam's Economic Entities in Transition*, edited by S. Sakata, 204–226. Basingstoke: Palgrave Macmillan.

Santiago, F. 2014. "Innovation for Inclusive Development." *Innovation and Development* 4 (1): 1–4.

Stiglitz, J. E. 2012. *The Price of Inequality*. New York, NY: WW Norton.

UNDP. 2014. *Inclusive Development*. New York, NY: UNDP. http://www.undp.org/content/undp/en/home/ourwork/povertyreduction/focus_areas/focus_inclusive_development/

World Bank. 2012. Introductory Note, presented at Regional Inclusive Innovation Policy Forum, Beijing, May 23–24.

World Bank. 2013a. *Shared Prosperity*. Washington, DC: World Bank. http://www.worldbank.org/en/news/feature/2013/05/08/shared-prosperity-goal-for-changing-world

World Bank. 2013b. *World Development Report 2014*. Washington, DC: World Bank.

How inclusive can innovation and development be in the twenty-first century?

Theo Papaioannou

Development Policy and Practice, The Open University, Walton, UK

Innovation is crucial for development. Addressing twenty-first century developmental challenges requires innovative processes and products, which help in reducing and/or eliminating the gap between rich and poor in the society. Such innovations can meet basic needs of low- and middle-income groups in developing countries, providing them with capabilities to function. The aim of this paper is to answer the question of how inclusive (of people and places) innovation and development can be in the twenty-first century. The paper therefore reviews new models of innovation for development, including 'frugal' and 'grassroots' or 'below the radar' innovation models. The argument put forward is that their inclusiveness depends not only on their diffusion to the poor but also on their generation according to principles of participation and equity derived from contemporary theories of global justice. These are conditions with direct impact on meeting the poor's basic needs and increasing their capabilities to function.

1. Introduction

Innovation and development are interrelated concepts. The former refers to developing new ways of doing things by mixing up ideas and/or combining technologies; the latter refers to changing people's conditions by removing various types of socio-economic, political and natural constraints, which leave them unfree to enjoy equal social relations and pursue the kinds of life they value. This interrelation between innovation and development has traditionally been approached in the context of the formal sector, i.e. the sector of socio-economic activities, which is formally regulated and included in gross domestic product (GDP). However, since the dawn of the new millennium, we have been witnessing a growing body of social and economic research that, on the one hand, demonstrates technological innovation in the formal sector fails to address the needs of the poor (Arocena and Sutz 2003; Arocena and Sutz 2012; Chataway, Hanlin, and Kaplinsky 2013; Cozzens 2007; Cozzens et al. 2005; Prahalad 2005; Smith, Fressoli, and Hernán 2013; Srinivas and Sutz 2008) and, on the other, identifies emerging models for creation of pro-poor products and services associated with the informal sector. These include 'frugal' innovations, i.e. simplified versions of existing technological products, and 'grassroots or below the radar' innovations (BRI), i.e. low- and middle-income group-generated innovations drawing on traditional knowledge and available technologies. A recent Organization for Economic Co-operation and Development (OECD) report brands them as 'inclusive innovations' arguing that they can contribute substantially to improving the welfare of the worst-off in developing countries (OECD 2012). In this sense, inclusive innovations begin to be understood not only as emerging factors of international development which succeed where the so-called Sussex Manifesto (SM) (Singer et al. 1970) and the Appropriate Technology Movement (ATM) (Schumacher 1973) failed,[1] but also as essential means of global justice which are able to meet twenty-first century challenges, such as deepening poverty and increasing health needs, in the global south.

The aim of this paper is to address the following question: how inclusive (of people and places) can innovation and development be given twenty-first century globalizing capitalism? In order to achieve its aim, the paper reviews emerging models of frugal and grassroots or BRI innovations from the point of view of global justice. It argues that the inclusiveness of such models in fact depends not only on their diffusion to the poor but also on their generation according to political principles of equity and participation. Taking such principles seriously has a direct impact on meeting the basic needs of the poor and increasing their capabilities to function.

The paper is divided into five sections. Section 2 critically analyses the concept of inclusiveness and its importance for evaluating innovation. In doing so, it draws on contemporary theories of global justice. Section 3 discusses in detail emerging models of innovation for development. Section 4 evaluates such models in terms of inclusiveness. Section 5 concludes that no innovation can be inclusive unless global justice principles of participation and equity are applied in the process of new product generation and diffusion.

2. The concept of inclusiveness and its importance for evaluating innovation

Before we address the question of inclusive innovation and development within twenty-first century capitalism, we should clarify the concept of inclusiveness. This concept has been traditionally defined as the opposite of social exclusion. However, although the latter has received tremendous attention since its introduction in the 1970s (De Haan 1997; Figueiredo and De Haan 1998; Gore and Figueiredo 1997; Jordan 1996; Rodgers, Gore, and Figueiredo 1995; Silver 1995) the former has been less popular with social scientists and political philosophers. One reason for this may be that the concept of inclusiveness is related to social equity, equality of opportunity and democratic participation. Thus, it presupposes a multi-dimensional theory of justice that incorporates all these principles. Such a theory is difficult to develop, given the preoccupation of political philosophy with fair distribution of income and wealth. Inclusiveness describes processes of equalization of resources, welfare or capabilities, which prevent people from becoming marginalized and deprived. Although, as Hickey and du Toit (2007) point out, the concept is not coterminous with poverty reduction, many poor people, especially in the developing world, are not included in (or are excluded from) the benefits offered by globalization. As Sen (2000, 2) explains,

> Globalisation is both a threat (especially to traditional ways of earning and living) and an enormous opportunity (especially in providing new ways of being prosperous and affluent). The ability of people to use the positive prospects depends on their not being excluded from the effective opportunities that globalisation offers (such as new patterns of exchange, new goods to produce, new skills to develop, new techniques of production to use, and so on).

Evidence suggests that countries of Sub-Saharan Africa (SSA) are less integrated than developed areas of East Asia, Europe and North America, with increasing global inequality (Martell 2007). Although SSA witnessed high rates of growth during the 2000s (almost 50% higher than the global average), the number of people living at or below US$1.25 per day increased by 59%.

Similarly, India despite its recent high growth rates, witnessed a further 42 million people living below the absolute poverty line (Chataway, Hanlin and Kaplinsky 2013).

This persistent exclusion of the poor across the globe has prompted contemporary cosmopolitan theorists[2], such as Pogge (2002), Beitz (2005), Caney (2005), Singer (2008), Nussbaum (2008) and Sen (2009), to argue convincingly that rich countries have obligations towards the poor. These obligations are founded upon the idea of global justice. Indeed, global justice obligations are more demanding than humanitarian aid. As Beitz (1975) argues, they require sacrifices on the part of the better-off and global institutional reforms. Cosmopolitans insist that principles of distributive justice with global scope should govern all processes of resource, welfare or capability allocation, including innovation and development. Inclusiveness can only come about through the application of such principles. Thus, for instance, in the field of health innovation, cosmopolitans such as Pogge (2002) propose expansion of the Rawlsian 'difference principle' and the 'equal right to basic liberty' in order to justify the political development of global institutions that can promote inclusive innovation and development. According to these principles '… social and economic inequalities are to be arranged so that they are both (a) reasonably expected to be to everyone's advantage and (b) attached to positions and offices open to all' (Rawls 1972, 60).[3] Although, as is well known (Papaioannou 2011; Papaioannou, Yanacopulos, and Aksoy 2009), in his *The Laws of Peoples*, Rawls (1999) strongly rejects the monism between the global and the domestic, Pogge (2005) insists that a global theory of justice can only be Rawlsian in its principles. Thus he proposes a global social structure guided by the difference principle and the equal right to basic liberty that can include institutions such as a Health Impact Fund (HIF), which would provide innovators with stable and financial incentives to address the needs of the poor.

It might be said that, in essence, Pogge advances an institutional solution to the problem of exclusive innovation and development. Especially in the case of the HIF, the purpose is to address two aspects of exclusiveness: the lack of equal access to essential medicines and the failure to develop innovative drugs for the poor. Both aspects manifest due to the lack of market demand in low-income countries (Prahalad 2005). For Pogge, the solution is an alternative intellectual property rights (IPR) system (what he calls the Patent 2 option) that operates in parallel to the current IPR system (what he calls the Patent 1 option) and that requires innovators to make public all information about their innovation. This makes them eligible for reward from an international HIF in proportion to the positive impact of their innovation on increasing health (i.e. inclusiveness) and decreasing poverty (i.e. exclusiveness) (Hollis and Pogge 2008).

As has been argued elsewhere (Papaioannou 2013) although Hollis and Pogge's institutional proposal for a HIF has been designed to promote inclusive innovation and proactive or creative equality (Arocena and Sutz 2003), it fails to do so in a number of respects. First, a HIF is based on the profit incentives argument that suggests innovation-generated inequality can be justified so long as it improves the lives of the worse-off. This argument accepts that inclusiveness can be unequal. In the case of Pogge's proposal, the more positive the impact of innovations on increasing health and decreasing poverty, the more reward for HIF innovators. Second, such a proposal is limited to health innovation. In this sense, it is narrow and cannot necessarily be extended to other areas of innovation for the poor. Third, a HIF is based on voluntariness. If big pharmaceutical companies fail to invoke the Patent 2 option, then this option would be like ' … unfinished monuments in the desert: testimonies to failed ambition' (Buchanan, Cole, and Keohane 2011, 20).

Cosmopolitans such as Buchanan, Cole and Keohane (2011) accept the importance of global justice for inclusive innovation but reject the extension of Rawls's principles to development of new global institutions such as a HIF. For them, positive rights of distributive justice can be legally enforced by international law (Papaioannou 2013). Non-Rawlsian cosmopolitans such as Buchanan, Cole, and Keohane (2011) propose to promote inclusive innovation and development through a Global Institute for Justice in Innovation (GIJI). Given that their concern is impediment to diffusion of innovation in general and not just health, these cosmopolitan thinkers argue that a GIJI would be an institution designed to construct and implement a set of policies governing the just and inclusive diffusion of innovations. This institution, in a similar way to the World Trade Organisation, would

> ... encourage the creation of useful innovations, for example through prizes and grants for justice-promoting innovations and through offering extended patent life for innovations that have a positive impact on justice. But its major efforts would be directed toward the wider and faster diffusion of innovations in order to ameliorate extreme deprivations and reduce their negative impact on basic political and economic inequalities ... (Buchanan, Cole, and Keohane 2011, 9–10)

One important asset of GIJI would be the possibility to authorize compulsory licensing of slowly diffusing innovations. Another asset would be the possibility of compensation through GIJI and not through royalties from the sales of licensed innovations.

It might be argued that, although both assets of GIJI are important, they do not go far enough to replace the current IPR system with new incentives for inclusive innovation and development. Neither compulsory licensing nor compensation through GIJI can lead to innovatively inclusive societies where all people and communities are given equal opportunities to participate in the generation of innovation and to access novel products and services. Science, technology and innovation can play crucial roles in improving the lives of poor people, making them better-off compared to their previous situation (Arocena and Sutz 2012; Juma et al. 2001; UNDP 2001). However, as has been argued elsewhere (Papaioannou 2013), even if we assumed that the assets of GIJI could promote inclusiveness of people and places in science, technology and innovation, they would face serious problems, such as the lack of political support from powerful industrialized countries, conflict of material interests and power relations in the global structure (Callinicos 2002; Rosenberg 1994).

2.1. *Sen and capabilities*

One powerful critique of both Rawlsian and non-Rawlsian proposals is Sen. Even though also a cosmopolitan thinker, in *The Idea of Justice*, Sen argues that

> Justice is ultimately connected with the way people's lives go, and not merely with the nature of the institutions surrounding them. In contrast, many of the principal theories of justice concentrate overwhelmingly on how to establish *just institutions* and give some derivative and subsidiary role to behavioural features. (Sen 2009, x–xi; italics added)

The inability of just institutions to deliver equity and participation lies in their top-down and formal character that fails to influence how people transform their 'primary goods', e.g. rights, liberties, income, wealth, etc. into specific functionings.

As has been pointed out elsewhere (Papaioannou 2013), Sen is more interested in just development than just innovation. This is because specific types of innovation constitute means of development and not ends in themselves. For Sen, the issue seems to be whether such innovations can substantially connect to basic capabilities, e.g. life, health, imagination, etc. and thereby to specific functionings, which people have reason to value. If so, then they can reduce injustice in development. The latter is a process of freedom that according to Sen (1999, 3) ' ... requires the removal of major sources of unfreedom: poverty as well as tyranny, poor economic opportunities as well as systematic social deprivation, neglect of basic facilities as well as intolerance or overactivity of repressive states'. For Sen, freedom is both the end and the means of development.

People ought to be capable of choosing the kind of life they (have reason to) value. Therefore, people have good reason to value not being excluded from innovations which can increase their capabilities. In a paper on 'Social Exclusion: Concept, Application and Scrutiny' Sen (2000, 4) argues that ' … capability deprivation can take the form of social exclusion. This relates to the importance of taking part in the life of community … '. From this argument it follows that the extent to which innovations are inclusive depends on their impact on people's capabilities for performing certain social functionings. In Sen's theory, capabilities as such are

> … sets of vectors of functionings … A functioning may be any kind of action performed, or state achieved, by an individual, and may a priori cover anything that pertains to the full description of the individual's life. Therefore, such a description may be done by a list or "vector" (or "n-tuple") of functionings. (Fleurbaey 2006, 300)

Sen does not allow for functionings that are not based on capabilities. Rather, he thinks that even if people are capable of certain functionings, it is up to them to choose whether they want to achieve them or not. Sen appears to give capabilities 'lexical priority' over functionings. The reason why he prioritizes capabilities over functionings is clear: by focusing only on achievements, one would miss the freedom dimension of human life. Thus, great achievements in terms of 'frugal' and 'grassroots or BRI' are in fact not so great if they take place in a totalitarian state of affairs that allows little or no space for freedom. Such innovative achievements are of limited or of no value.

Certainly, Sen's capability approach has received criticism (Clark 2006) as regards the problem of disagreement about the valuation of capabilities (Beitz 1986), the high informational requirements of the system (Alkire 2002) and the paternalistic way of determining capabilities for low-income developing countries. However, despite criticism, this approach has been endorsed by global policy organizations in the area of innovation and development, including the United Nations, the World Bank and even the International Monetary Fund (Pieterse 2010). The strength of the capabilities approach is first of all that it is flexible, allowing theorists and policy-makers to apply it in different ways (Alkire 2002). Second, the capability approach neither puts forward a fixed index of capabilities nor presupposes one social context within which to assess individual advantage. Third, this approach does not claim to be a complete theory of justice or inclusive development, recognizing the need for incorporation of other principles, including growth and efficiency (Clark 2006). Fourth, and more importantly, the capability approach does not impose an institutional solution to the problem of inclusive innovation and development. In this sense, it allows for new models of innovation to be evaluated in terms of their contribution towards preventing capability deprivation.

Although the capability approach is a strong normative candidate for evaluating new models of innovation in terms of inclusiveness, it seems to have a crucial weakness: it assumes liberal cosmopolitan politics and structures for its implementation. Recent evidence from political sociology suggests that there is no basis for such politics (Martell 2011). Cosmopolitanism as a theory of global justice politically fails to promote inclusiveness on the ground. Our critique here endorses recent political arguments according to which ' … cosmopolitan ethics may be requiring non-cosmopolitan politics' (Martell 2011, 621).[4] These arguments do not necessarily raise doubts about cosmopolitanism as a normative approach to global justice and inclusiveness but do criticize it as a political approach to equity and participation. Cosmopolitanism in general and Sen's theory of capabilities in particular tend to view politics in terms of common global consciousness of problems such as the growing gap between rich and poor. Therefore, they pursue equity (of capabilities) and (democratic) participation as global solutions negotiated and agreed at cosmopolitan forums and top-down institutions, e.g. the World Trade Organisation. However, as Martell (2008, 131) points out

> ... such global consciousness is unlikely. One reason for doubt is the lack of empirical evidence for it. Powerful nations sometime opt out of shared consciousness or action or make the problem worse. They put economic or national interests before ... common consciousness.

Indeed, it might be argued that equity and participation are egalitarian principles which cannot be pursued and achieved through consensus at top-down political institutions. Equity and participation aim at ending socially imposed oppression and at guiding the formation of a community in which people stand in social and political relations of equality to others (Anderson 1999). This aim goes far beyond equalization of capabilities through cosmopolitan politics and towards local expression of equal respect and concern for all citizens. Equity ought to be social and political while participation ought to be democratic. To put it another way, both principles oppose hierarchies (including innovation hierarchies) promoting ' ... collective self-determination by means of open discussion among equals, in accordance with rules acceptable to all' (Anderson 1999, 313). Global negotiations of, and agreements on these egalitarian principles, through top-down political institutions, are impossible due to power, inequality and conflict relations (Martell 2008). This is even more so in the area of innovation and development where established hierarchies and dominant value chains reproduce inequality (Cozzens and Kaplinsky 2009) and conflict at the expense of human rights (Juma 2013). What is possible globally is an understanding of the conflicts involved over innovation and development issues.

2.2. Basic needs approach

It might be suggested that emerging innovation models in low- and middle-income countries have to be evaluated through an alternative non-institutional framework that assumes local politics (as opposed to liberal cosmopolitanism politics). In a series of papers (Papaioannou 2011, 2013), I have defined such a framework as public action and campaigning for satisfying basic human needs in an equitable and participatory way. According to Reader (2006, 337)

> The "basic needs approach" (henceforth BNA) is an approach to social justice that gives priority to meeting people's basic needs – to ensuring that there are sufficient, appropriately distributed basic needs (BN) goods and services to sustain all human lives at minimally decent level. BNA draws on the intuitive moral force of claims of need (compared to claims of preference or subjective or objective benefit, for example) to develop a practical normative theory about what should be done.

This approach does not require the overoptimistic establishment of new global structures such as HIF and GIJI. More importantly, it does not presuppose consensus on basic needs to be achieved through negotiations at cosmopolitan forums and top-down institutions. Rather, the basic needs approach (BNA) assumes conflict and alliances taking place in the bottom-up processes of clarifying basic needs.

Although it is true that the BNA has been criticized and eventually overshadowed by capability theory in the early 1990s, it is also true that this approach can be revisited today for the purpose of evaluating emerging models of innovation in terms of inclusiveness. Human needs as such are instrumental. As Wolff (2009, 215) points out, ' ... needs are always needs for something. But for what? Presumably for the elements of a flourishing life'. It might be said that the very basic elements of a flourishing life are the same for all human beings and their societies. These elements are both natural (life, nutrition, health, etc.) and social (political freedom, housing, education, etc.). Natural and social basic needs are interrelated. For instance, health is often determined by education, housing, etc.

It might be argued that interrelated natural and social needs can be considered as alternative evaluative criteria of inclusive innovation. The focus here is not just on the outputs of innovation, i.e. equity in the distribution of new goods and services that satisfy basic needs, but also on the process of innovation, i.e. participation in the generation of those new goods and services for basic needs. The advantage of using basic needs as alternative evaluative criteria of inclusive innovation is not only that those criteria are less abstract and more pragmatic than capabilities but also that capabilities as such presuppose satisfaction of basic needs. People remain unable to choose certain functionings unless basic natural and social needs are satisfied. Equal satisfaction of basic needs implies equal freedom from fundamental natural and social constraints. Therefore, each individual's ability to choose the life he/she wants to live depends on this type of negative freedom. Agreement on and elaboration of an index of basic needs can be only achieved through democratic participation in particular developmental contexts and communities. This takes the form of equal involvement in decision-making and implies a bottom-up process of politics that is different from the top-down process of cosmopolitan politics. The latter is centralized, global and consensus politics while the former is decentralized, local and conflict politics.

The *Universal Declaration of Human Rights* in Article 25 provides a general approach to basic needs by stating that 'Everyone has the right to a standard of living adequate for the health and well-being of himself and of his family, including food, clothing, housing and medical care and necessary social services … ' (UN 1948). This rights-based approach to basic needs also includes another crucial dimension of social justice, namely recognition of the poor. As Fraser and Honneth (2003) point out, claims for recognition increasingly become crucial because they are put forward together with claims for redistribution of resources and/or capabilities. 'In the redistribution paradigm, the remedy for injustice is economic restructuring of some sort … In the recognition paradigm … the remedy for injustice is cultural or symbolic change' (Fraser and Honneth 2003, 13). In the case of inclusive innovation, redistribution might involve policy changes towards equalizing resources and incentives for frugal, grassroots or BRI to meet basic needs while recognition might involve upwardly revaluing disrespected identities of pro-poor innovators (Papaioannou 2013).

Innovations can be inclusive of people and places as long as they can satisfy basic needs in an equitable and participatory way. From this it follows that emerging models of innovation cannot be branded as inclusive unless there is evidence of equal satisfaction of basic human needs in specific developmental contexts. This evidence should not only concern the diffusion of emerging innovations but also their generation. It might be argued that the inclusiveness of the former depends on the inclusiveness of the latter. This argument reconstructs Marx's position that 'Any distribution whatever of the means of consumption is only a consequence of the distribution of the conditions of production themselves' (Marx 2000, 616). If the conditions of generating innovations are not equitable and participatory (e.g. bottom-up, equally involving the poor and taking on board their needs), then the final products, no matter how innovative they are, will be exclusive of the poor and their basic needs. The possibility of inclusive innovation in twenty-first century globalizing capitalism depends on whether the very generation of new products and services allows bottom-up processes of equity and participation to determine the basic needs they will satisfy.

3.   New models of innovation for development

So far this paper has clarified the concept of inclusiveness and defended its importance for evaluating emerging innovation models in terms of basic needs. But how should we understand these models for development? In 2009, a group of innovation and development researchers led by Raphael Kaplinsky at the Open University recognized that dominant paradigms of Mode 1 and Mode 2 innovation[5] in high-income countries either ignore the basic needs of consumers in low-income countries or lack the technologies and organizational structures to address these needs effectively. In 2010, the STEPS Centre at the Institute of Development Studies published *A New Manifesto* confirming that

> ... expenditure on research and development across developing countries has risen to approximately 1% of aggregate GDP. Yet outside the emerging innovation centres in rapidly industrialising econom-ies, levels of research and development as a percentage of GDP remain at around 1970 levels in some countries – especially in part of Africa. (STEPS Centre 2010, 6)

Both Kaplinsky et al. (2009) and the STEPS Centre (2010) demonstrate that dominant innovation paradigms based on rent-seeking firms which introduce new products and processes have been exclusive of the poor.

In response to dominant paradigms of exclusive innovation, new emerging firms and value chains are likely to reduce poverty and disrupt global hierarchies of innovation (Kaplinsky et al. 2009). Such firms begin to engage poor people at the bottom of the global income pyramid (BoP) as both consumers and producers who actively participate in driving innovation and growth. The incentives of BoP-serving firms are often reactionary to perceived social injus-tice in dominant innovation paradigms. Certainly, as a recent report by the Harvard Corporate Social Responsibility initiative points out, the number of 'inclusive businesses' in developing countries is still low due to systemic challenges, such as low levels of education, poor infrastruc-ture and regulatory systems (Gradl and Jenkins 2011). Nevertheless, as the OECD (2012) stresses, such emerging models of innovation for or by low- and middle-income groups are essential for inclusive growth. In what follows we take a closer look at these models.

3.1. *Frugal innovation*

The term 'frugal innovation' was introduced in India to describe attempts to cut out the luxury and unnecessary features of high-tech products developed for high-income markets (Chataway, Hanlin and Kaplinsky 2013). This new model of innovation has been conceptualized as 'inno-vation for low- and middle-income groups' (OECD 2012, 30). Given that frugal innovations are often lower quality versions of more sophisticated technological products and processes, they allow the poor to buy them at affordable prices, meeting some basic needs and increasing welfare benefits. The OECD has listed a number of cases of frugal innovations. However, for the purpose of this paper, let us focus on two of them.

Case 1: Computer-based Functional Literacy (CBFL) in India. This is an innovation inspired by the high percentage of poor people who are illiterate in India. The Tata Group has developed the CBFL technique to teach an illiterate individual to read in a fraction of time, only 40 h of training, at US$2 per individual. This technique is innovative in that it involves animated graphics and a voiceover that explains the relationship between alphabets, structure and meaning of important everyday words. CBFL has so far helped more than 20,000 poor people learn to read and the ambition is for the technique to become available for agriculture and health-care teaching.

Case 2. Money Maker Irrigation Pump (MMIP) in Kenya. This innovation was designed by the KickStart International non-governmental organization (NGO), and has been used by some poor Kenyan farmers at a cost of US$100. This foot-powered pump costs less than a diesel pump and can irrigate up to two acres of land per day. MMIP has helped a number of poor farmers to move from rain-fed agriculture to irrigated farming, boosting their annual income by US$1000 and increasing crop diversity. KickStart estimates that it has helped to lift more than 400,000 people out of poverty.

Both cases of frugal innovation are driven by demand for cheap products. However, they do not necessarily meet basic education and food needs, as the recent OECD report implies (OECD 2012). The fact that there are differences between lower and higher income groups in terms of demand for such frugal innovations is mainly due to price constraints and not to basic needs. The determining role of cost is also reflected in the cheap modification of products such as mobile handsets and handheld electrocardiograms by north-based transnational companies (TNCs), such as Nokia and General Electric. The objective of these TNCs is not widening access per se but profit from low-income markets with via economies of scale. Indeed, according to OECD (OECD 2012, 37), the promise is that ' ... of accessing new growing markets, such as India and China with their enormous populations. Because even the middle class in such countries has comparatively low incomes, efforts to provide lower-cost alternatives can be attractive'. Given this fact, the argument that demand for frugal innovations reflects basic needs is only partly correct. Some basic needs for quality food and good education can simply not be met by cheap 'low tech' or modified innovations. As will be argued in the next section, inclusiveness is a multi-dimensional concept that cannot be realized if people are offered low-quality products. This might explain why in particular developmental contexts people resist being included as consumers of cheap and low-quality innovations.

3.2. *Grassroots or BRI*

This is another emerging model of innovation that has been conceptualized by OECD as 'innovation by low- and middle-income groups' (OECD 2012, 30). In grassroots or BRI, lower income groups are not just the target consumers but also the innovative producers. This implies that by drawing on indigenous knowledge and relevant technologies and by forming powerful networks of activists, practitioners and organizations, lower-income groups introduce innovations solving practical problems in local communities and meeting basic needs. These innovations might represent incremental changes in existing technological products (Bhaduri and Hemant 2009). However, as has been argued elsewhere (Kaplinsky et al. 2009, 191),

> ... a key feature of BRI is the *collective significance* of these various developments underlying innovation as a process. The likelihood, therefore, is for the development of new products in China and India aimed at these low-income markets. The product-process linkage inherent in many sectors ... leads to a clustering of production technologies which are similarly reflective of operating conditions in these low-income markets.

Apart from the large value of grassroots or BRI for low-income local communities, such innovations are considered to be potentially disruptive of global innovation hierarchies. This is not so much because of the introduction of new technologies but because of the new types of consumers who induce grassroots or BRI. As has been stressed elsewhere (Kaplinsky et al. 2009, 192) the existing innovation leaders

> ... are unable to either recognise or exploit these new opportunities. Their trajectories and market antennae inhibit them from fully recognising these new opportunities which are "below the radar". Their cost structure – with regard to not just their core component technologies, but also the structure of their value chains – makes it difficult to address these markets, even if they are recognised.

The OECD (2012) and also Smith et al. (2012) have listed a number of cases of grassroots or BRI. However, for the purpose of this paper, we have selected the following two.

Case 3. Grassroots or BRI through the Honey Bee Network (HBN). A number of innovations, including pedal-powered washing machine, groundnut digger, multi-crop thresher, cotton stripper, etc. have emerged in communities at the bottom of the pyramid. The HBN, founded by Anil Gupta, has identified and documented such grassroots innovations while the National Innovation Foundation (NIF) in India has tried to scale them up, applying them to solve similar problems elsewhere. Different methods of information gathering have been used, including active attempts to look for community-based innovations and traditional knowledge. Walking through Indian villages and holding village meetings are some of these methods. The central argument has been that poor people have always been relying on their own ingenuity to solve their problems away from high-technology innovation systems, which are based on research and development (R&D).

Case 4. Grassroots or BRI through the Social Technologies Network (RTS) in Brazil. A number of innovations, including portable water storage, biodigesters for home energy, solar dryers or solar desalters, socio-participatory certification, community gardens, etc. have provided solutions for social inclusion and improvement of livelihoods. These innovations are not only characterized by simplicity and low cost but also by ability to generate income and improve the quality of life of local communities leading to development. They are re-applicable in the sense that they can be recreated and appropriated by local populations (Smith et al. 2012). RTS in Brazil comprises more than 800 public institutions, social movements and NGOs. The main goals of this network are democratization, accessibility and continuous improvement. This implies a normative and political agenda, rejecting control and hierarchies in generating innovative products and promoting creativity of producers and consumers. Grassroots or BRI through RTS in Brazil are based on the recognition that hierarchical technological patterns of the neo-liberal north and profit-seeking innovation, what is often termed 'the Schumpeterian motor' (Chataway, Hanlin and Kaplinsky 2013) have so far led to innovation exclusion and poverty. Instead, grassroots or BRI through the RTS can promote inclusiveness involving local communities and transferring their knowledge and innovations to other populations. These are counter-hegemonic technological patterns, which can generate income and employment from communities, social movements and organizations.

Both cases of grassroots or BRI are driven not only by demand for cheap problem-solving products but also by normative and political principles of equity and participation. Indeed these innovations are crucial in terms of empowering local communities to meet their basic needs. In India, as Bhaduri and Hemant (2009) argue, intellectual inspiration for grassroots innovations can be traced back to the teachings of Mahatma Gandhi and Rabindranath Tagore who supported a need-based approach to technology. This is the reason why they are developed and scaled up through local networks and not-for-profit organizations of NGOs. As Chataway, Hanlin and Kaplinsky (2013, 22) confirm, such networks and organizations ' … remain a considerable source of inclusive innovation today, even though much of this occurs "BRI" and does not surface in many of the measures used to measure innovation such as patents, R&D, sales and trade'.

Grassroots networks and social movements are driven by local initiatives that often challenge social and political structures of marginalization and exclusion, pushing for change (see Fressoli et al. this special issue). As Smith, Fressoli and Hernán (2013, 2) point out

Grassroots innovation is an explicitly normative agenda, which seeks to mobilise distinctly political processes, such as claims to social justice, and often questions organisational and economic assumptions in conventional innovation policies. Alternative initiatives tend to arise in civil society and solidarity economy arenas, where groups experiment with social innovations as well as developing "appropriate technologies" responsive to local situations and needs.

The politics of grassroots innovation is predominantly non-cosmopolitan, going from the bottom-up, based on local community initiatives rather than institutional top-down, assuming cosmopolitan ideals.

4. Evaluating innovation and development in terms of inclusiveness

As has been already pointed out, the OECD (2012) and a number of researchers (Chataway, Hanlin and Kaplinsky 2013; Dutz 2007; Kaplinsky et al. 2009; Lorentzen 2010; Smith et al. 2012) regard new models of innovation for development as inclusive models without providing a normative theory or a clear evaluative framework of innovation inclusiveness. Therefore, the question that still remains open is this: How one can understand and/or evaluate (and even measure) frugal and grassroots or BRI in terms of inclusiveness? To answer this question we should revisit our earlier discussion of the concept of inclusiveness and stress that it is not a politically neutral concept. That is to say, what inclusive innovation means within liberal politics of development is different from what it means within non-liberal politics of development. For liberals, inclusive innovation might be translated as the formal right of everyone to be included in market processes and outcomes. For non-liberals, inclusive innovation might be translated as the substantive and equitable participation of everyone in innovation processes and outcomes, which are not necessarily market led.

Revisiting our earlier criticism of the liberal cosmopolitan approach to inclusive innovation provides us with a good basis for applying or operationalizing our suggestion that the BNA might in fact be a more plausible framework of evaluation. The argument for this suggestion has been that the BNA is a non-institutional framework allowing for new models of innovation such as frugal and grassroots or BRI to be evaluated in terms of their contribution towards satisfying natural and social needs. Given that equity and participation constitute essential criteria of this evaluative framework, the question that arises is to what extent specific cases of frugal innovation (i.e. cases 1 and 2) and specific cases of grassroots of BRI (i.e. cases 3 and 4) satisfy both criteria, meeting equitable needs and improving participation.

To begin with cases 1 and 2, existing evidence suggests that neither CBLF nor MMIP are equitable and/or participatory innovations. Both frugal innovations come at a price that, by definition, excludes those who live below the Millennium Development Goal of US$1.25 per day. The absolute poor in India and Kenya who are unable to purchase CBFL and/or MMIP are unable to meet their need to learn reading/writing skills and/or to improve their farming techniques. In cases 1 and 2, frugal innovations promote inequitable inclusiveness of people and places. This is because they clearly exclude the poorest. CBFL and MMIP cannot be seen as a means of development for everyone. In addition to this, they are not participatory innovations. There is no evidence to suggest that poor consumers were involved in their conception and production. Rather, the Tata Group in India and the KickStart International NGO in Kenya introduced these frugal innovations as rent-seeking enterprises, which can better understand local markets and use locally available resources. In fact, CBFL and MMIP remain 'innovations from above' (Chataway, Hanlin, and Kaplinsky 2013), which fail to meet any basic needs of those on the lowest incomes, and which fail to meet the participatory needs of those outside the elite innovatory clique.[6] The same holds for other frugal innovations such as ultralow-cost mobile handsets, solar energy systems for the poor, low-cost word processing, e-mail devices, etc. None of these innovations are absolutely inclusive of poor consumers and places, let alone satisfying the principles of equity and participation in processes and outcomes.

Moving on to cases 3 and 4, existing evidence suggests that both HBN and RTS may be participatory networks but not necessarily equitable. These networks include innovators such as farmers and entrepreneurs, policy-makers, academics and NGOs committed to identifying and rewarding innovative ideas and traditional knowledge produced at the grassroots level by poor citizens and their communities. Interaction between communities and technology developers leads to adopting and benefiting from grassroots or BRI. However, benefits are not always equally distributed between poor consumers given existing power relations within their communities and wider socio-political structures of inequality. In addition, there are high transaction costs of identification and documentation of grassroots or BRI, and low commercialization prospects. But, despite problems of equity, grassroots or BRI are more likely to satisfy basic needs than frugal innovations. This is for two reasons: first of all, grassroots or BRI are less exclusive of the poorest, i.e. those who live below US$1.25 per day. The absolute poor in India and Brazil are able to use some of the HBN and RTS innovations provided they have a connection to these networks. To put it another way, grassroots or BRI promote collective empowerment for meeting local needs. Through networks such as HBN and RTS, innovation and development cease to be the privilege of specific individuals and begin to include the whole community.

Certainly, more rigorous investigation and critical insights are necessary in order to show how grassroots or BRI contribute to improving the livelihoods of people in low-income communities. In addition, questions also need to be raised about the possibility of such innovations in high-income countries. This is because, as Hernán and Fressoli (2011, 14) stress,

> social exclusion is not circumscribed to under-developed countries; it is merely more apparent and seems crueller there. However, observing the shortcomings of healthcare systems, the social integration problems and the environmental risks that riddle the so-called "developed" countries, as well as the restriction in access to goods and services, is enough to notice the inability of the market economy to solve key social issues.

Grassroots or BRI might be able to remedy specific market failures in developed countries, replacing innovations that exacerbate social problems.

Despite substantial differences between frugal and grassroots or BRI, in fact, all these emerging innovations are able to help poor people to satisfy some basic needs or, to use Sen's terminology, achieve some basic functionings under certain conditions. The question is what should the role of public policy be vis-à-vis such innovations? Should public policy support frugal innovations in some contexts (e.g. in communities living above US$1.25 and below US$2.50 per day) and grassroots or BRI in some other contexts (e.g. in communities living below US$1.25 per day)? The answer may be in the positive given the nature of basic needs of these different communities. Public policy should be first concerned with satisfying such needs through frugal and grassroots or BRI, and then with increasing capabilities. As has been stressed earlier in this paper, increasing capabilities presuppose satisfying basic needs. Public policy focused on both industrial and social development can provide combined institutional and financial support to those frugal and grassroots or BRI, which can satisfy basic needs. This support can range from provision of incentives for inclusive innovation to reduction of instabilities and insecurities of frugal and grassroots or BRI innovators. The establishment of NIF in India seems to be one good example. This is an autonomous organization supported by India's Department of Science and Technology. NIF's objective is to strengthen grassroots innovations and traditional knowledge. So far it is claimed that NIF has built a database of more than 1,060,000 innovations and has filed over 550 patents on behalf of innovators. The Brazilian Ministry of Science and Technology (MCT) is another example. MCT supports several social technology projects, aiming to improve the functionings of poor agricultural and urban populations. Only in 2004, it is claimed that, MCT spent R$10 million on agricultural projects and in 2005 R$32.2 million went to 278 projects of grassroots or BRI. However, as Smith et al. (2012) observe, attempts to link the mainstream innovation community with grassroots innovation movements remain embryonic. Despite the support of MCT and the Brazilian innovation agency (FINER), RTS has so far failed to engage R&D institutions and universities. This not only suggests 'indifference or even resistance' from the country's scientific and political elites but also an epistemological, moral and political gap between such elites and grassroots social movements. Scientific and political elites reproduce and/or strengthen the dominant and hegemonic paradigm of innovation because their survival depends on it. By contrast, grassroots innovation communities promote an alternative and counter-hegemonic paradigm that is potentially disrupting of local and global innovation and political hierarchies.

Whatever the outcome of this social and political struggle, one thing is certain: unless public policy supports frugal and grassroots or BRI, which contribute towards meeting local basic needs, a number of community-generated technologies might fail the same way that 'appropriate' and 'intermediate' technologies failed in the 1970s and 1980s. Yet this support should not necessarily be institutional. Public policy should rather avoid developing more formal/cosmopolitan institutions of innovation. Our research suggests that such global institutions rarely have a BNA-based vision. This explains why they can fail particularly in supporting grassroots innovation. On the other hand, unless a BNA-based vision can move emerging innovation models beyond the local and towards disrupting existing global innovation hierarchies, frugal and grassroots or BRI are also bound to decline.

5. Conclusion

This paper has sought to address the question of inclusive innovation under twenty-first century capitalism. It did so by proposing a non-institutional framework of basic needs focused on the political principles of equity and participation. This framework prioritizes inclusiveness of processes over inclusiveness of outcomes on the grounds that the former presupposes the latter. Emerging models of innovation, such as frugal and grassroots or BRI, can be evaluated as inclusive to the extent that they can satisfy both principles, meeting peoples' basic needs through non-cosmopolitan politics. Otherwise, they can be thought of as innovations that have no positive impact on inclusiveness. The current academic discussion on inclusive innovation avoids taking a clear normative position or promoting a plausible evaluative framework. Revisiting the basic human needs approach to inclusiveness might close this normative gap. In any case, evaluating emerging models of innovation in terms of needs might provide strong justification for public policy support of frugal and grassroots or BRI in both developing and developed countries.

Notes

1. Both the SM and the ATM failed to change the dominant paradigm of innovation. Technological progress remained a predominantly hierarchical and exclusive process located in the north. On the one hand, the SM only spoke to a very specialized audience of innovation experts in developed countries. On the other hand, the ATM turned science and technology elites in developing countries against 'economically inefficient' appropriate technologies, often perceived as an attempt to lock such countries into low productivity and undynamic techniques (Kaplinsky 2009, 2011).
2. Cosmopolitanism is a global political theory that maintains ' ... that there are moral obligations owed to all human beings based solely on our humanity alone, without reference to race, gender, nationality, ethnicity, culture, religion, political affiliation, state citizenship, or other communal particularities' (Wallace Brown and Held 2010, 1). This implies a notion of common humanity that translates ethically into an idea of common moral duties towards others. Cosmopolitanism puts forward three normative commitments: individualism (i.e. the primary units of moral concern are individuals, not states); equality (i.e. the moral concern for individuals should be equally applied to all); and universality (i.e. all humans are equal in their moral standing as if they are all citizens of the world). Although the

origins of cosmopolitan thought can be traced back to Immanuel Kant (2008), twenty-first century chal-lenges of globalization, including the spread of infectious diseases and the threat of climate change, remind us that events in one part of the world have impact on people in other parts of the world and therefore give contemporary relevance to cosmopolitanism.

3. For Rawls, justice demands equal sharing of liberty and opportunity, income and wealth, and self-respect. This does not imply elimination of all inequalities but only those which put someone in a worse-off situation. In Rawls's theory 'If certain inequalities benefit everyone, then they will be accepted by everyone' (Kymlicka 1990, 53). This theory is illustrated in his two principles of justice. The 'equal right to basic liberty' implies that each individual has the right to equal share of resources. The 'difference principle' tell us that inequalities in sharing resources are morally justified only in so far as they are to everyone's advantage. To put it another way, unless such inequalities put someone in a worse-off position, they are morally justified.

4. Non-cosmopolitan politics means politics away from global fora and cosmopolitan institutions. Such institutions often constitute arenas of clashing interests, and values which are dominant in the west but fail to promote economic and political development in poorer countries. Non-cosmopolitan politics promotes social democracy at state level and international alliances locally. This implies a conflict approach to politics (as opposed to consensus or agreement between political actors at the level of cos-mopolitan institutions) taking into account clashing material interests and power (Martell 2011). Collab-oration can be mainly established locally with those actors who have similar ideological and material interests.

5. The concepts of Mode 1 and Mode 2 innovation were introduced by Gibbons et al. (1994) to charac-terize and theorize the transition from scientific knowledge production based on disciplinary and exper-imental research to scientific knowledge production based on interdisciplinary and reflexive research. The latter involves much more stakeholder interests and capacities than the former (Kaplinsky 2009). Mode 2 has come to dominate the innovation process in high-income economies of the north. By con-trast, low-income economies of the south are still embedded in Mode 1 innovation, failing to involve poor consumers and other stakeholders.

6. This clarification was suggested by one of this journal's reviewers. I would like to thank him/her for the contribution.

References

Alkire, S. 2002. *Valuing Freedoms: Sen's Capability Approach and Poverty Reduction*. Oxford: Oxford University Press.

Anderson, E. S. 1999. "What Is the Point of Equality?" *Ethics* 109 (2): 287–337.

Arocena, R., and J. Sutz. 2003. "Inequality and Innovation as Seen from the South." *Technology in Society* 25: 171–182.

Arocena, R., and J. Sutz. 2012. "Research and Innovation Policies for Social Inclusion: An Opportunity for Developing Countries." *Innovation and Development* 2 (1): 147–158.

Beitz, C. R. 1975. "Justice and International Relations." *Philosophy and Public Affairs* 4 (4): 360–389.

Beitz, C. R. 1986. "Amartya Sen's Resources, Values and Development." *Economics and Philosophy* 2 (2): 282–291.

Beitz, C. R. 2005. "Cosmopolitanism and Global Justice." *The Journal of Ethics* 9 (1/2): 11–27.

Bhaduri, S., and K. Hemant. 2009. "Tracing the Motivation to Innovate: A Study of Grassroots in India." Papers on Economics and Evolution 0912. http://hdI.handle.net/10419/32660

Buchanan, A., T. Cole, and R. O. Keohane. 2011. "Justice in the Diffusion of Innovation." *The Journal of Political Philosophy* 19 (3): 306–332.

Callinicos, A. 2002. "Marxism and Global Governance." In *Governing Globalisation*, edited by D. Held and A. McGrew, 249–266. Cambridge: Polity.

Caney, S. 2005. *Justice Beyond Borders: A Global Political Theory*. Oxford: Oxford University Press.

Chataway, J., R. Hanlin, and R. Kaplinsky. 2013. "Inclusive Innovation: An Architecture for Policy Development." IKD Working Paper 65, The Open University. Accessed January 13, 2014. http://www.open.ac.uk/ikd/documents/working-papers/ikd-working-paper-65.pdf

Clark, D. A. 2006. "Capability Approach." In *The Elgar Companion to Development Studies*, edited by D. A. Clark, 32–45. Cheltenham: Edward Elgar.

Cozzens, S. 2007. "Distributive Justice in Science and Technology Policy." *Science and Public Policy* 34 (2): 85–94.

Cozzens, S. E., K. Bobb, K. Deas, S. Gatchair, A. George, and G. Ordonez. 2005. "Distributional Effects of Science and Technology-based Economic Development Strategies at State Level in the United States." *Science and Public Policy* 32 (1): 29–38.

Cozzens, S. E., and R. Kaplinsky. 2009. "Innovation, Poverty and Inequality: Cause, Coincidence or Co-evolution?" In *Handbook of Innovation Systems and Developing Countries: Building Domestic Capabilities in a Global Setting*, edited by B.-A. Lundvall, K. J. Joseph, C. Chaminade, and J. Vang, 57–82. Cheltenham: Edward Elgar.

De Haan, A. 1997. "Poverty and Social Exclusion: A Comparison of Debates on Deprivation." Working Paper 2 Poverty Research Unit. Sussex, Brighton: University of Sussex.

Dutz, M. A. 2007. *Unleashing India's Innovation: Toward Sustainable and Inclusive Growth*. Washington, DC: World Bank.

Figueiredo, J. B., and A. De Haan, eds. 1998. *Social Exclusion: An ILO Perspective*. Geneva: International Labour Organisation.

Fleurbaey, M. 2006. "Capabilities, Functionings and Refined Functionings." *Journal of Human Development* 7 (3): 299–310.

Fraser, N., and A. Honneth. 2003. *Redistribution or Recognition? A Political-Philosophical Exchange*. London: Verso.

Gibbons, M. C., H. Limoges, S. Nowothy, P. Schwartzman, P. Scott, and M. Trow. 1994. *The New Production of Knowledge: The Dynamics of Science and Research in Contemporary Societies*. London: Sage.

Gore, C., and J. B. Figueiredo. 1997. *Social Exclusion and Anti-Poverty Policy*. Geneva: International Labour Organisation.

Gradl, C., and B. Jenkins. 2011. "Tackling Barriers to Scale: From Inclusive Business Models to Inclusive Business Ecosystems. Harvard Kennedy School Corporate Responsibility Initiative." Accessed January 13, 2014. http://www.hks.harvard.edu/m-rcbg/CSRI/publications/report_47_inclusive_business.pdf

Hernán, T., and M. Fressoli. 2011. "Technologies for Social Inclusion in Latin America: Analysing Opportunities and Constraints; Problems and Solutions in Argentina and Brazil." Accessed January 13, 2014. https://smartech.gatech.edu/bitstream/handle/1853/42606/657-1817-2-PB.pdf

Hickey, S., and A. du Toit. 2007. "Adverse Incorporation, Social Exclusion and Chronic Povery." CPRC Working Paper 81. Accesed May 12, 2014. http://www.chronicpoverty.org/uploads/publication_files/WP81_Hickey_duToit.pdf

Hollis, A., and T. Pogge. 2008. "The Health Impact Fund: Making New Medicines Accessible for All." Accessed January 13, 2013. www.incentivesforglobalhealth.org

Jordan, B. 1996. *A Theory of Poverty and Social Exclusion*. Oxford: Blackwell.

Juma, C. 2013. "Technological Innovation and Human Rights: An Evolutionary Approach." Working Paper, Harvard Kennedy School.

Juma, C., K. Fang, D. Honca, J. Huete-Perez, V. Konde, and S. H. Lee. 2001. "Global Governance of Technology: Meeting the Needs of Developing Countries." *International Journal of Technology Management* 22 (7/8): 629–655.

Kant, I. 2008. "Perpetual Peace." In *The Global Justice Reader*, edited by T. Brooks, 319–331. Oxford: Blackwell.

Kaplinsky, R. 2009. "Schumacher Meets Schumpeter: Appropriate Technology Below the Radar." IKD Working Paper 54. Available at: Kaplinsky, R. 2011. "Bottom of the Pyramid Innovation and Pro-poor Growth." IKD Working Paper No. 62. Accessed January 13, 2014. www.open.ac.uk/ikd/publications/working-papers

Kaplinsky, R. 2011. "Bottom of the Pyramid Innovation and Pro-poor Growth." IKD Working Paper 62. Accessed January 13, 2014. www.open.ac.uk/ikd/publications/working-papers

Kaplinsky, R., J. Chataway, N. Clark, R. Hanlin, D. Kale, L. Muraguri, T. Papaioannou, P. Robbins, and W. Wamae. 2009. "Below the Radar: What Does Innovation in Emerging Economies Have to Offer Other Low-income Economies?" *International Journal of Technology Management & Sustainable Development* 8 (3): 177–197.

Kymlicka, W. 1990. *Contemporary Political Philosophy: An Introduction*. Oxford: Clarendon Press.

Lorentzen, J. 2010. "Low Income Countries and Innovation Studies: A Review of Recent Literature." *African Journal of Science and Technology, Innovation and Development* 2 (3): 46–81.

Martell, L. 2007. "The Third Wave in Globalization Theory." *International Studies Review* 9 (2): 173–196.

Martell, L. 2008. "Beck's Cosmopolitan Politics." *Contemporary Politics* 14 (2): 129–143.

Martell, L. 2011. "Cosmopolitanism and Global Politics." *The Political Quarterly* 82 (4): 618–627.

Marx, K. 2000. "Critique of the Gotha Programme." In *Karl Marx: Selected Writings*, edited by D. McLellan, 610–616. Oxford: Oxford University Press.

Nussbaum, M. C. 2008. "Capabilities as Fundamental Entitlements: Sen and Social Justice." In *The Global Justice Reader*, edited by T. Brooks, 598–614. Oxford: Blackwell.

OECD. 2012. "Innovation and Inclusive Development, Conference Discussion Report." Accessed April 29, 2013. http://www.oecd.org/sti/inno/oecd-inclusive-innovation.pdf

Papaioannou, T. 2011. "Technological Innovation, Global Justice and Politics of Development." *Progress in Development Studies* 11 (4): 321–338.

Papaioannou, T. 2013. "Innovation and Development in Search of a Political Theory of Justice." IKD Working Paper 63. Accessed January 13, 2014. http://www.open.ac.uk/ikd/documents/working-papers/ikd-working-paper-63.pdf

Papaioannou, T., H. Yanacopulos, and Z. Aksoy. 2009. "Global Justice: From Theory to Development Action." *Journal of International Development* 21 (1): 805–818.

Pieterse, J. N. 2010. *Development Theory.* London: Sage.

Pogge, T. W. 2002. *World Poverty and Human Rights: Cosmopolitan Responsibilities and Reforms.* Cambridge: Polity Press.

Pogge, T. 2005. "Human Rights and Global Health: A Research Programme." *Metaphilosophy* 36 (1–2): 182–209.

Prahalad, C. K. 2005. *The Fortune of the Bottom of the Pyramid: Eradicating Poverty Through Profits.* Upper Saddle River, NJ: Pearson Education/Wharton School Publishing.

Rawls, J. 1972. *A Theory of Justice.* Oxford: Oxford University Press.

Rawls, J. 1999. *The Law of Peoples.* Cambridge, MA: Harvard University Press.

Reader, S. 2006. "Does a Basic Needs Approach Need Capabilities?" *The Journal of Political Philosophy* 14 (3): 337–350.

Rodgers, G., G. G. Gore, and J. B. Figueiredo, eds. 1995. *Social Exclusion: Rhetoric, Reality, Responses.* Geneva: International Institute for Labour Studies.

Rosenberg, J. 1994. *The Empire of Civil Society.* London: Verso.

Schumacher, E. F. 1973. *Small Is Beautiful: A Study of Economics as If People Mattered.* London: Blond & Briggs.

Sen, A. 1999. *Development as Freedom.* Oxford: Oxford University Press.

Sen, A. 2000. "Social Exclusion: Concept, Application and Scrutiny." Social Development Papers 1, Office of Environment and Social Development Asian Development Bank. Accessed January 13, 2014. http://housingforall.org/Social_exclusion.pdf

Sen, A. K. 2009. *The Idea of Justice.* London: Penguin.

Silver, H. 1995. "Reconceptualising Social Disadvantage: Three Paradigms of Social Exclusion." In *Social Exclusion: Rhetoric, Reality, Responses*, edited by G. Rodgers, C. Gore, and J. Figueiredo, 57–80. Geneva: International Institute for Labour Studies.

Singer, P. 2008. "Famine, Affluence and Morality." In *The Global Justice Reader*, edited by T. Brooks, 387–396. Oxford: Blackwell.

Singer, H., C. Cooper, R. C. Desai, C. Freeman, O. Gish, S. Hill, and G. Oldham. 1970. *The Sussex Manifesto: Science and Technology to Developing Countries During the Second Development Decade.* New York: United Nations.

Smith, A., E. Arond, M. Fressoli, T. Hernán, and D. Abrol. 2012. "Supporting Grassroots Innovation: Facts and Figures." SciDev. Accessed January 13, 2014. http://www.scidev.net/en/science-and-innovation-policy/supporting-grassroots-innovation/features/supporting-grassroots-innovation-facts-and-figures-1.html

Smith, A., M. Fressoli, and T. Hernán. 2013. "Grassroots Innovation Movements: Challenges and Contributions." *Journal of Cleaner Production.* Accessed January 13, 2014. http://www.sciencedirect.com/science/article/pii/S0959652612006786

Srinivas, S., and J. Sutz. 2008. "Developing Countries and Innovation: Searching for New Analytical Approach." *Technology and Society* 30 (2): 129–140.

STEPS Centre. 2010. *Innovation, Sustainability, Development: A New Manifesto.* Brighton: STEPS Centre.

UNDP. 2001. *Human Development Report 2001: Making New Technologies Work for Human Development.* Oxford: Oxford University Press.

United Nations. 1948. "The Universal Declaration of Human Rights." Accessed January 13, 2014. http://hdr.undp.org/sites/default/files/reports/262/hdr_2001_en.pdf

Wallace Brown, G., and D. Held. 2010. *The Cosmopolitan Reader.* Cambridge: Polity Press.

Wolff, J. 2009. "Disadvantage, Risk and the Social Determinants of Health." *Public Health Ethics* 2 (3): 214–223.

Regulating the negative externalities of enterprise cluster innovations: lessons from Vietnam

J.J. Voeten[a] and W.A. Naudé[b]

[a]Tilburg School of Economics and Management, Tilburg University, Tilburg, The Netherlands;
[b]Maastricht School of Management, UNU-MERIT, and University of Maastricht, Maastricht, The Netherlands

Innovation has been acknowledged as contributing to development, in particularly inclusive innovations that involve and benefit poorer groups in developing countries. However, such innovations may have negative externalities. Most often external regulation is required to reduce these effects. However, it is often not enough, and in many developing countries the required institutional context is not present to enable external regulation. Hence, a case may be made for internal regulation of inclusive innovation. Helping to fill the gap in our knowledge on internal regulation of innovation externalities in developing countries, we explore four cases of innovation in informally organized small producers' clusters Vietnam. From this we propose a model of internal regulation as a societal process.

1. Introduction

Innovation can be broadly defined as the process of introducing new processes, new products and new business concepts that create value (Nelson and Winter 1977; Kline and Rosenberg 1986) and as the 'putting into practice of inventions' (Fagerberg, Mowery, and Nelson 2005). Widely used measures of innovation such as R&D expenditure and patent filings suggest that innovation is concentrated in advanced economies (Szirmai 2008). However, taking an understanding of innovation in a broader sense – including as the (incremental) introduction of new processes, existing products in different markets and/or changes in business practices – innovation may be seen to be widely prevalent in developing countries (Wolf 2007; Gellynck, Kühne, and Weaver 2011; Szirmai, Naudé, and Goedhuys 2011). Indeed, a small but growing literature has been concerned to describe the nature and extent of innovation and growth in developing countries, in particularly innovations that involve and benefit poorer groups. Various typologies have been introduced – frugal innovation, jugaad innovation and Base of the Pyramid (BOP) innovation – including 'inclusive innovation'; the particular focus here (Utz and Dahlman 2007; Zeschky, Widenmayer and Oliver 2011; George, McGahan and Prabhu 2012; Radjou, Prabhu and Ahuja 2012).

Despite this rising interest in innovation in developing countries, it is still the case that innovation is overwhelmingly seen as having only positive impacts on growth and development. The fact is, however, that innovation does not always or automatically result in unambiguous development. Cozzens and Kaplinsky (2009) state that growth does not necessarily reduce poverty and 'about half the time inequality decreases with growth and half the time it increases with growth'. Moreover, innovation may also be marked by negative externalities. These include direct and indirect costs, including environmental and societal, that result from innovation and that affect otherwise uninvolved actors and stakeholders. This means that, a priori, poor people may not necessarily always participate in or benefit from innovation, even supposedly inclusive innovation. As Soete (2012, 7) posed it, 'Could it be that innovation is not always good for you?'

One way of addressing negative externalities that may be associated with innovation is by institutionalizing policy and regulatory frameworks. Soete (2012), for instance, argues for better public sector surveillance and regulation. Such 'external' regulation, important though it is, is not the only possible approach, particularly in developing countries where the formal institutional context is often weak. Furthermore, external regulation of innovation is subject to the problem of asymmetric and imperfect information; by definition innovation results in novelty, and the longer term impacts of these novelties may not always be known to external regulators. Innovative entrepreneurs may be able to avoid detection, taxation, or effective regulation, even in advanced economies with established institutions, as the global financial crisis of 2008 made painfully clear. In developing countries, the often weaker formal institutional structures may further hamper a prompt assessment of harmful outcomes and the establishment of external regulation mechanisms. In most fragile states, government 'capture' by innovative entrepreneurs and other business interest groups is the norm.

The shortcomings of external regulation of innovation in developing countries suggest that 'internal' forms of regulation may be more necessary than the literature had until now recognized. By 'internal' regulation, we mean mechanisms through which an entity (e.g. firm) exercises control over itself (Palzer and Scheuer 2003). In the case of innovation, for instance, to monitor economic, social and environmental innovation consequences and responses of customers, employees, shareholders and stakeholders (Hart 2009). An example of this is the recent move of large corporations to adopt voluntary internal and industry-level regulation mechanisms, such as corporate social responsibility (CSR) programmes or sets of global ethical standards (e.g. the UN Global Compact or the Organisation for Economic Co-operation and Development (OECD) Guidelines for Multinational Enterprises).

In contrast, most of the inclusive innovation by smaller, informal entrepreneurs in developing countries – which mostly goes unnoticed by the scholarly community – may or may not be subjected to internal regulation, as very little is known about this at present. The result is that there is only a limited understanding of the broad spectrum of innovation outside of the large multinational and state-owned firms, and a lacuna in terms of the internal regulation mechanisms to limit or avoid negative spillovers from these other forms of innovation. Yet, these 'other forms' – particularly inclusive innovation by small and micro-enterprises based on lower income communities – are increasingly recognized as central to socio-economic development (Utz and Dahlman 2007; Soman, Stein, and Wong 2014).

The contribution of this paper is to argue that these internal regulation mechanisms may also be important in developing countries to limit the negative impacts of innovation by smaller indigenous firms. We do this by presenting case studies from informally organized clusters of small producers in Vietnam, explored in earlier research on responsible innovation (Voeten et al. 2012). The cases contain various critical elements of inclusivity in terms of poverty alleviation (Alkire 2007; London 2007; World Bank 2008), accessibility to and empowerment of the poor (Sen 1999) and acknowledging responsibility for negative innovation externalities (Elkington 1999; Hart 2007). Vietnam is an interesting context for this study, being a notable example of a fast-growing economy as a result of economic reforms and increasing integration into the global economy while at the same time suffering considerable environmental degradation as well as persistent poverty. The rest of the paper will proceed as follows. In Section 2, we provide the theoretical context, and in Section 3 we set out our methodology. The various cases we discuss are presented and analysed in Section 4. We conclude with discussing implications for promoting inclusive innovation for development.

2. Theoretical context

2.1. *Innovation in developing countries*

The growing interest in innovation in developing countries stems from the idea that basic improvements in innovation and technology infrastructure can contribute to improvements in welfare, education, and productivity in economic sectors (Aubert 2005). However, the institutional environment is characterized by the presence of high transaction costs and by weak institutions (Collier 1998). These affect the functioning of the market and the transmission of signals – e.g. demand for certain goods – to the innovators. As a consequence of the overall problematic environment, innovation systems in developing countries are poorly constructed. Given their relatively lower innovative capacities, developing countries are generally dependent on industrialized countries for the provision of new technology and knowledge (Léger and Swaminathan 2007).

These positions resulted in 'stylized facts' of innovation in developing countries: (i) productivity and economic growth are largely resource- and factor-driven, and not innovation-driven; (ii) innovation tends to be of the 'new to the firm' rather than the 'new to the world' variety, i.e. imitative in nature; (iii) innovation tends to be incremental rather than radical or disruptive and (iv) national innovation systems, a prerequisite for high and sustained innovation-driven growth, are largely lacking in developing countries (Szirmai, Naudé, and Goedhuys 2011).

These 'stylized facts' have recently come under scrutiny. There may be more 'innovation' in developing countries than that is captured in traditional measures such as R&D. A newly emerging consensus recognizes that while innovation is important at all stages of a country's economic development, different innovation manifestations may play different roles at various stages. In earlier stages in developing countries, incremental innovation is often associated with the adoption of foreign technology, imitative innovation and introduction of new combinations; it does not involve technological breakthroughs (OECD 2012). Mobile telephony in Africa is a frequently used example. In fact, a number of studies have found evidence for the contribution of innovation at the firm level to foster greater productivity and efficiency in developing countries. For instance, Van Dijk and Sandee (2002) describe patterns of innovation adoption and diffusion in the Kenyan food processing sector, furniture making in Nicaragua and tile manufacturing in Indonesia. They find that these innovation efforts resulted in improved entrepreneurial performance. Gebreeyesus (2011) discusses innovation and micro-enterprise growth in Ethiopia. And a growing body of research documents the innovativeness of small and medium-sized firms in the developing countries' information and communications technology (ICT) and other hi-tech sectors (Dutz 2007).

Unpacking these studies shows that 'early stage' innovation takes place in developing countries but often materializes in a different – less visible – way. Moreover, the innovation process often does not manifest solely at the firm level but materializes in networks or clusters of enterprises, which have been acknowledged for their collective efficiency (Schmitz, 1999) and dynamism and links to wider global markets (Caniëls and Romijn, 2007; Szirmai, Naudé and Goedhuys 2011). The notion of innovation occurring within a larger constellation of actors is familiar in the more developed economies; being referred to as innovation systems (Lundvall 1992), learning networks (Watts and Strogatz 1998) and learning regions (Rutten and Boekema 2007). But the particular interest here is the poor, informal context in developing countries and the innovations occurring within clusters of small and micro-enterprises. Given the lack of attention to such cluster-based innovation within lower income communities, we can see this as a model of inclusive innovation that requires greater emphasis and exposure; with the specific focus of this paper, as discussed next, being the impact of this form of innovation.

2.2. *Innovation as two-edged sword*

Richard Feynman once quoted a Buddhist proverb stating that 'to every man is given the key to the gates of heaven; the same key opens the gates of hell'. Innovation and entrepreneurship have the same two-sided nature. Nuclear energy, the automobile, guns and modern medicine are all cases in point. As a result, authors have pointed to the fact that innovation can have negative, undesirable consequences for the economic development process (Soete 2012). Hence, and also in developing countries, one has to acknowledge the possible harmful societal consequences of innovation, which may conflict with broader development goals.

Negative externalities of innovation related to development have not been addressed much in the literature. However, there is a small but growing body of scholarly work that encompasses such externalities in economic, social and environmental spheres (Ferreira and Ravallion 2009; World Bank 2012). Examples include unfavourable or even dangerous working conditions (e.g. in recycling of heavy metals used in ICT), jobless growth (e.g. through automation of services) and environmental damage through pollution or degradation of ecosystems (e.g. over-fishing due to the use of more efficient nets).

In addition to the negative spillover effects of innovations, Baumol (1990) pointed to the impact of 'destructive' entrepreneurship. His point is that when entrepreneurs innovate, it is to improve their 'own status and wealth'. This can, however, come at a cost to the rest of society (Soete 2012; Desai, Acs and Weitzel 2013; Sanders and Weitzel 2013).

Where communal/institutional mechanisms to regulate entrepreneurship and its related innovations are lacking, these types of negative externality of innovation are costs borne by society or by others, not by the entrepreneurs. There is, therefore, the danger of a 'dark side' to inclusive innovation – not merely that poor people in developing countries may fail to benefit from the innovations being undertaken in their context; but that they may suffer the costs of such innovations through environmental degradation, social inequalities and economic stagnation. One implication is that innovation impacts must be understood through a lens that sees not just income but also a broader, multi-dimensional understanding of development encompassing capabilities, equality and sustainability (Sen 1999; Elkington 1999; Hart 2007; Gries and Naudé 2011). The second implication is that innovation must be understood not just as a process to be set free but also as a process that needs some regulation; a topic to which we now turn.

2.3. *Regulation*

A common economic perspective in dealing with negative externalities is to argue for control and regulation (policy). As a result, environmental and social policies and regulations have been developed and implemented, but with varying degrees of success. As noted in Section 1, this external form of regulation suffers from problems of asymmetric information; it is also becoming increasingly costly (Levi-Faur 2005) while simultaneously the power of the nation-state to regulate is facing erosion in a globalizing world (Cioffi 2000). These challenges are often multiplied in developing country settings given the weaker foundation of formal institutions.

As also noted in Section 1, the alternative to external regulation is internal regulation by enterprises and innovators themselves. There is already a sizeable set of both activity and literature on this in the context of the global North, where internal regulation has seen the development of notions such as CSR (Bowden 1953; Frederick 1960), the stakeholder approach (Freeman 1984), and sustainable business and the 'people–planet–profit' triple bottom line (Elkington 1999; Hart 2007). While there may be concerns about the motivations behind such initiatives, this type of internal regulation is seen as a complement to – and perhaps even a substitute for – external, government regulation, which faces the challenges just identified (Parker 2002; Palzer and Scheuer 2003).

These trends in internal regulation have so far largely been studied in the cases of multinational firms and large indigenous or state-owned firms in developing and emerging economies. There is a gap in the literature on the internal regulation of innovative entrepreneurs in micro, small and medium, informal and family-owned firms in developing countries. We know next to nothing about the forms such internal regulation may take, nor about the extent to which the possible negative impacts of their innovative activities may be circumvented or reduced. In the remainder of the paper, we seek to help fill this lacuna, by discussing and analysing a number of case studies from Vietnam, focusing specifically on internal regulation of innovative enterprise clusters.

3. Method and background

3.1. *Method*

We analysed inclusive innovation along with its societal impacts in four craft villages[1] in the Red River Delta in northern Vietnam. These were chosen for three main reasons. First, because they reflect the model of cluster-level innovation noted above, rather than just firm-level innovation; with cluster-based innovation being a notable manifestation of innovation in the Vietnamese context (as concluded in earlier research: Voeten, de Haan and de Groot 2011). Second, because they reflect the notion of inclusivity. The village enterprises are generally informal sector; that sector being where 60% of those on lower incomes find employment. Although the impact of each individual household micro-enterprise is small, as a cluster they are much more significant; being equivalent in production size and employment creation to a large enterprise. Vietnamese enterprise clusters provided direct employment to an average of 2000 people per village and many more indirectly. (Of course they were also comparable to large enterprises in terms of their negative externalities, as discussed later.)

The third reason for selection was that these craft villages were exemplars of a wider phenomenon. In the Red River Delta alone, there are 300 such villages (Nguyen, Tran, and Le 2003). The selected four were found to be similar to the broader population in terms of size, structure, geographical location, type of enterprise and innovation, and their institutional, economic and political context. In total, it is estimated that there are 1500 such villages in the whole of Vietnam (Konstadakopulos 2005).

The four particular villages were selected in order to provide a variety of different innovation externalities, and community perceptions and responses to those externalities. Over a period of three years, we carried out a series of 7 to 10 data collection visits per village[2]. We interviewed (open interviews) some 20 to 30 households per village to discuss innovations and the negative innovation externalities leading to societal conflicts, and conducted 20 further interviews of village administration officers, clients, tourists and transportation sector workers. We analysed the data and identified patterns and impacts of innovation through an iterative process involving theoretical analysis and comparison. This *grounded theory* approach (Glaser and Strauss 1967) enabled us to inductively develop an understanding of the nature of innovation and the emerging innovation externalities. Moreover, conducting a series of visits over time made it possible to observe the changes and social dynamics in the villages in terms of emerging harmful consequences, how the various actors perceived these and responded, how conflicts emerged and whether eventually regulation of the harmful outcomes was taking place.

3.2. *Vietnam*

Over the past two decades, Vietnam has become an emerging economy in Southeast Asia after many troubled years, including a war with the USA, and hardships during a socialist post-reunification era. In 1986, Vietnam initiated an economic reform campaign (*Doi Moi*), setting in motion a transition process that would shift the economy from its socialist orientation towards a free and more open market economy, integrating into the global economy. Since *Doi Moi*, the Vietnamese economy has experienced considerable growth. In 1986, Vietnam was listed among the poorest countries in the world with a per capita gross domestic product (GDP) of US$203. GDP growth averaged 7.8% per annum over the period from 1995 to 2008 and has quadrupled since the reforms (IMF 2008).

Rapid growth brought about new societal challenges. Wages for low-skilled jobs are minimal and unemployment is high. Economic growth has benefitted urban more than rural households, resulting in a growing income disparity (Cling, Razafindrakoto, and Roubaus 2011). Other challenges include environmental degradation, lack of diversification in production and exports, and a declining contribution of productivity growth to economic growth and poverty reduction (World Bank 2012). Pollution is a significant problem; some of the rivers and lakes in urban areas are little more than open sewers, and levels of heavy metal and other industrial pollutants are well above safe levels in some areas.

Large multinational firms, domestic large firms and state-owned firms as well as households are important causes of these negative environmental effects (World Bank 2012). Inevitably however, small and micro-firms are also responsible for the simple fact that they play a significant role in Vietnam's economy in terms of number of businesses, employment creation and contribution to GDP. In 2007, the informal sector accounted for almost 11 million jobs out of a total of 46 million, with, as noted above, those jobs being disproportionately directed at those on lowest incomes (Cling, Razafindrakoto, and Roubaus 2011). Informality constitutes a growing feature of many developing countries, and notwithstanding its heterogeneity, the informal sector is generally associated with low profits and productivity, limited credit access, the absence of official employment contracts and limited or no social security for workers (Rand and Torm 2012). However, the informal sector should not be associated with stasis. Many informal enterprises have been going through an innovation trajectory in a process of product and service upgrading. This is most evident in the case of micro- and household-based crafts businesses in the country.

In the course of the agricultural collectivization in the 1950s, private sector activities were restricted and craft villages were converted into cooperatives. With the introduction of the economic reform policy in 1986, the people in the craft villages faced the challenge of re-organizing their networks and, where appropriate, adjusting their production to modern market demands. New markets were made accessible and some craft villages changed their production – in other words, they have been increasingly innovative to adjust to the new global economic challenges facing the country. We now turn to an analysis of these craft villages to study the link between the impact of their innovation and internal regulation mechanisms.

4. Case studies

4.1. *Van Phuc silk village*

Van Phuc is a semi-urban craft village 12 km south-west of Hanoi specialized in silk weaving. The silk industry village was collectivized in the socialist command economy and silk products were sold to state-owned intermediaries. After the introduction of the free market economy in the 1990s, silk weaving households innovated by adopting new marketing routines, as well as by opening retail shops in the village's main street; a functional innovation assuming responsibility for the marketing function in the value chain. This resulted in an increase in demand for silk weaving, and stimulated further home-based silk production – boosted by an increase in tourism to the village. Overall silk production in Van Phuc has tripled and sales in small shops account for 40% of overall sales.

By and large the village benefitted from the advantage of the new marketing practices. The silk weavers and silk dye workshops in the village enjoy higher and more stable incomes than before, albeit not to the same extent as the shop owners. Competition is increasing and the shops have to compete more on price and/or produce a differentiated product. The former implies the need for higher production volumes per business and also pressure not to keep costs to a minimum. The latter implies a need to produce designs that meet current fashions.

Although the silk shops do not affect the environment directly, increased silk production in Van Phuc has caused serious environmental problems, particularly water pollution. The weaving workshops and shop owners outsource the dyeing to several specialized workshops in the village. The latter use more toxic chemicals for the dyeing process to obtain fashionably bright colours. The wastewater from this process is discharged directly into the sewage system and river without any treatment. According to many villagers, this results in severe pollution, black river water and increased, and new, health problems.

The villagers began to see the result of the increased use of chemicals to create fashionable colours: severe water pollution and skin diseases. However, there were different internal understandings of whether this was caused by increased silk production or not. There are many polluting new factories around the villages. There is a growing mood in the village that the pollution is a problem that violates people's right to live in a safe environment. However, the general attitude among the small producers and shop owners is that the problem is an acceptable trade-off for increased economic prosperity. The dye workshop owners do not want to take any action to change their practices or increase their costs. The small producers assume that pollution in Van Phuc can only be addressed by the government and that it is the government's responsibility to do something about it.

4.2. *Duong Lieu cassava products village*

In the cassava-noodle-producing craft village Duong Lieu, groups of households traditionally processed cassava tubers into starch as an intermediate product, and sold it to other groups of households producing noodles within the village. Recently, several households introduced a product innovation in the form of new end products made from starch: children's candy, medicine pills and soft drinks. The candy production in particular has been quite a successful innovation. Candy production involves much lighter and quieter work, in contrast to the harder and dirtier tasks associated with starch and noodle production.

Candy production adds more value to the processing of cassava starch than noodle production. The sweets are sold at a 'good' price to agents in Hanoi who distribute them to new profitable markets within Vietnam, such as shops, mini-markets and super markets. They compete with imported sweets and provide the households with higher overall sales revenues than from noodles.

There is also an emerging pollution problem in the village. New end products have increased the demand for starch, resulting in more organic waste being discharged into the open sewage system. Several government research centres and non-governmental organizations have carried out environmental studies in Duong Lieu, which indicate a worrying pollution of soil and surface water associated with newly emerged health problems in the village, such as eye diseases and pneumonia. It is clear to all villagers that the solid organic waste pollution is a negative innovation externality that comes from the increased cassava starch production. However, the many small producers ignore these reports and they do not want to discuss the negative consequences with outsiders, including journalists and researchers. Nobody complains because they see the trade-off that this inconvenience is compensated by the economic outcomes of the innovation.

4.3. *Phu Vinh rattan and bamboo village*

For decades, the craft village Phu Vinh has produced traditional bamboo and rattan articles, including baskets, bins, plates and boxes for the domestic market. Some 10 years ago, villagers who had migrated to study in Hanoi and were looking for new income, established export companies around the village and successfully initiated exports to the USA and Europe.

The export companies outsource the orders to middlemen in the village who subsequently engage small producers for the actual production. The small producers do the weaving and deliver the semi-finished rattan and bamboo products to the middlemen and export companies who then do the final colouring and varnishing, as the last step before shipment overseas. This marketing innovation implies a significant shift to producing higher quality and more expensive rattan and bamboo products with a large increase in value created.

For the export companies and middlemen it is very profitable business. However, the innovation has worked to the disadvantage of the small household enterprises. They get a lower unit price, have to work harder and more family members are now involved in the production work – including children who work after school and old people – and they still earn less than before. This negative innovation externality is driving the small producers into poverty, they say, and making them feel marginalized.

The export companies take a hard-line business attitude and do not see that they have a role to play or a responsibility to modify unit prices to reduce poverty. They see poverty alleviation as the role of the government. The small-scale producers have a different view and blame the export companies for offering such low prices, arguing that they could share more of their profits. The bargaining power of the export companies is very strong indeed. The household rattan producers have no other options but to do business with the export companies. The village administration recognizes and sympathizes with the problems of poverty faced by the small-scale producers, yet feels unable to interfere with the economic process and the free market price-setting mechanism. There are more and more disputes and frictions between the export companies and the household producers.

4.4. *Bat Trang ceramics village*

Bat Trang is a ceramics and pottery craft village. In the old days, small producers in the cluster baked ceramic products in traditional pottery kilns, fired with wood and charcoal. The smoke emissions from the traditional charcoal kilns produced a lot of air pollution, causing many cases of respiratory diseases. Dirty storage areas for charcoal polluted the streets. At that time, reports identified Bat Trang as one of the more polluted craft villages in the Red River Delta. Some 10 years ago, a collective concern for a clean environment surfaced. Small producers innovated by introducing new kiln technology based on firing with liquefied petroleum gas (LPG).

Better control of baking temperatures combined with more intense heat resulted in the production of thinner and smoother ceramics with fewer defects. The new technology also allowed a broad variety of contemporary and popular types, shapes, colours and designs of ceramics to be produced. The new technology enables higher production volumes, higher quality ceramics (which can be exported) and saves on energy costs. The innovators have created surplus value in the village and new employment opportunities for poorer people.

The new production process has led to a significant improvement in the village's living environment. The LPG kilns emit less pollution than the charcoal kilns. Today the air is much cleaner and there are fewer dirty storage areas for charcoal in the streets. According to the villagers, the village is now a greener and a more pleasant place to live.

There is a collective concern for a clean environment. All community members see the clear link between the innovation and the cleaner air, and act accordingly. The discussions in the village about the societal implications have come about naturally because the inhabitants of Bat Trang feel strongly connected through family ties and their shared history in ceramic production. In this sense, the innovation process was a collective process and the villagers recognized their responsibility, rather than looking to the government for a solution. They have sought little external assistance to help them move forward.

5. Analysis and discussion

Table 1 summarizes the empirical material in terms of the introduction of new products, new processes and business practices in the Vietnamese cases identified as innovation (Voeten, de Haan, and de Groot 2011). Typically we identify one key innovation starting off a process of introducing other forms of newness. All the types of innovations are classified according to the typology of innovations[3] developed by Kaplinsky and Morris (2001).

The key innovations were new for the village concerned but not new to the world. The innovations mostly involved copying, imitating, adapting and adopting from technology elsewhere. The innovations were incremental, path dependent and did not concern radical technological breakthroughs, except for the LPG kiln in the Bat Tang ceramics case to a certain extent. In all cases, the innovation process was initiated, managed and owned by entrepreneurs themselves, which is critical in notions of poverty alleviation and (inclusive) development with regard to capability, participation and ownership (Sen 1999; Alkire 2007; London 2007).

The innovation process did not take place at the firm level but constituted an interactive process in which various small producers within the cluster participated. All cases show that the development of the innovation idea, the testing and the commercialization was a shared and interactive process among the small producers' households. Hence, we conceptualize these new dynamics as 'cluster-level' innovation rather than 'firm-level', the usual unit of analysis in Western-based definitions of innovation (OECD 2005). The innovators confirmed that the

Table 1.   Types innovations in the four villages.

Village	Key innovation	Type of innovation	Other newness
Van Phuc (silk):	Retail shops: the producers take over the marketing function of other value chain actors by setting up retail shops	Functional innovation	New silk products, new clients
Duong Lieu (cassava):	New products: the change from noodle to candy and other new end products	Product innovation	New technology
Phu Vinh (bamboo and rattan):	New markets: the export companies started to enter markets in USA and Europe	Market innovation	New products, new production processes
Bat Trang (ceramics):	New technology: introduction of LPG-fired kilns	Process innovation	New products, new shops

cluster provided a context for the innovation process in terms of cooperation, trust and information, and that this enabled learning and shared risk taking; all critical elements in the innovation process (Dosi 1988). The cluster in an informal way exerted several institutional functions comparable to an innovation system (Lundvall 1992).

All innovations created value for the cluster as a unit of analysis. In Bat Trang, Van Phuc and Duong Lieu, a broad group of poor small producers confirmed the increase in incomes. In Phu Vinh, however, there was emerging conflict within the cluster about the internal distribution of the innovation benefits, which was not considered equal and fair; small producers in the bamboo and rattan case did not appropriate value and got poorer instead, while the export companies in the cluster enjoyed good profits. In addition, as summarized in Table 2, there were other negative externalities described in the cases resulting from the innovation and conflicting with sustainable or inclusive development notions. There were also notable differences in the responses.

In Van Phuc, there was some acknowledgement of the negative environmental and health outcomes, but there were disagreements about attribution: whether silk production was the root cause. In Duong Lieu, the villagers did make the cause–effect connection that the increase in cassava starch production was causing the increasing amounts of waste and pollution. But this was accepted as a 'price worth paying' given the growth in incomes. In Phu Vinh, all villagers agreed that the poverty was a negative innovation externality resulting from the new export marketing practice. The export companies, however, do not acknowledge responsibility. There are no intervening third parties – government – and it has become an ongoing conflict. In Bat Trang, the air pollution perceived by all as a negative externality became unacceptable in the village. The producers acknowledged responsibility and introduced cleaner, LPG-fired kilns.

The Van Phuc, Duong Lieu and Phu Vinh cases correspond with the 'tragedy of the commons' concept of Hardin (1968) concerning the depletion of a shared resource by individuals, acting independently and rationally according to each one's self-interest, despite their understanding that depleting the common resource is contrary to the group's long-term best interests. The Bat Trang case, in which the individuals do take initiative and ownership by themselves, is in line with the ideas of Ostrom et al. (1999) that a tragedy of the commons is possible to avoid, once locals come up with solutions to the commons problem themselves. This is therefore an example of the internal regulation – within the cluster – of a negative externality of inclusive innovation.

In terms of conceptualizing internal regulation, the responses show a pattern of several steps of understanding and agreeing on the negative externality, considering it as a trade-off, or

Table 2. Negative externalities and responses.

	Negative externality	Responses
Van Phuc (silk)	Increased use of chemicals: severe water pollution and skin diseases	Difficulty in understanding and agreeing on the negative externality
Duong Lieu (cassava)	Solid organic waste dumped in sewage systems and open air. New diseases	Agreement on the negative externality and accepting it as trade-off
Phu Vinh (bamboo and rattan)	Unequal distribution of innovation incomes within the village. New poverty	Agreement on the negative externality but innovators do not acknowledge responsibility. Third-party enforcement required
Bat Trang (ceramics)	Charcoal kiln caused smoke and respiratory diseases	Agreement on the negative externality and innovators acknowledge responsibility

innovators accepting responsibility. Comparing the perceptions and responses from the case material in more detail, we advance a model (Figure 1) of approaching the internal regulation of the negative innovation externalities as a dynamic and interactive societal process of five steps. The model draws on the concept of *responsible innovation* – acknowledging responsibility for harmful outcomes – further developing and refining the ideas of Voeten et al. (2012). Our construction starts with the actual perception of societal change within the community and the issue of whether the change is harmful or not (step 1). Once the societal change is perceived and agreed as a problem, the community considers its origin; specifically, whether it is an innovation externality. At a certain point, the community understands and agrees whether societal change is a consequence of the innovation or not (step 2). Passing through these societal process steps implies a critical mass within the community, the tipping point (Gladwell 2000), that shares understanding and agrees on the issues at hand regarding the negative innovation externality. If it concerns an explicit negative externality, the subsequent question is whether this is an acceptable trade-off or an emerging issue (step 3). If it is not an acceptable trade-off, the next issue is whether the innovators acknowledge responsibility or behave opportunistically (step 4). If the innovators behave opportunistically, the conflict is likely to escalate, with no other solution than external regulation. If there are no third parties or existing institutional arrangements to enforce the innovator to acknowledge responsibility, there will be ongoing conflicts (step 5). In Figure 1, we identified an overall sequence (i) the agreement about the innovation externality, (ii) internal regulation and (iii) external regulation. If there is successful internal or external regulation (the space in the diagram above the dotted line), we termed the outcome of this societal process as what can be termed the 'inclusive innovation zone'.

6. Promoting internal regulation

When confronted with negative externalities, government agencies typically react through regulatory measures. These are often *evidence-based* (Howlett and Ramesh 1995; Nutley, Davies, and Smith 2000) and based on the assumption that the outcomes of actors' behaviour can be anticipated and manipulated by providing incentives, disincentives ('polluter pays') and an enabling regulatory framework.

However, the observation in the Vietnamese innovation cases and the proposed societal process model of regulation (Figure 1) does not match this type of approach with its evidence-

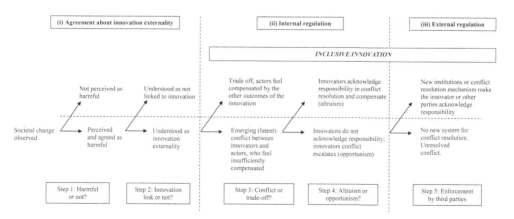

Figure 1. Conceptualizing regulation of inclusive innovation externalities as a societal process. Developed from Voeten et al. (2012).

based approach to policy-making, and its narrow focus just on formal enterprise innovation and a firm-level conception of negative externalities. The Vietnamese clusters show cluster-level innovation; no single enterprise is actually the owner of the innovation or sole originator of the negative externalities. Targeting the individual enterprise through a 'polluter pays' policy principle is therefore difficult. Another issue is the implicit claim, *ceteris paribus*, of understanding causalities between input – policy and institutional context – and the outcomes and behaviour of economic actors.

However, in the Vietnamese villages it is not possible to readily predict what course the societal process will take – whether externalities will result in societal conflict or not and whether they will be resolved internally. The analysis reveals a dynamic as well as complex societal process involving context-specific responses of community members who assess and value the outcomes and consequences of innovation against their own local normative frameworks. This fits critique of the evidence-based approach to policy-making on the grounds that it does not pay sufficient attention to the complexity and dynamism of practical realities, to emerging perceptions and upcoming constraints (Sanderson 2002; Nill and Kemp 2009).

Indeed, the perception of negative externalities may vary considerably from village to village. What is acceptable in one village may be the cause of conflict in another. A macro-policy approach therefore, assuming *one size fits all*, will probably not lead to effective regulation. The Vietnamese cases and the societal process model suggest context-specific internal regulation as an avenue to explore further; in particular, the idea of innovators acknowledging responsibility through interaction with other actors within the community. The model identifies an 'internal regulation phase' before establishing external regulation mechanisms, which has operational advantages in terms of fewer organizational costs while promoting community participation.

The challenge in operational terms is to provide support to a community to move swiftly through the stages of the societal process towards (i) agreement about innovation externality then subsequently to enable the community to come to an (ii) internal regulation situation. This implies that a community should be supported to assess and agree the harmful societal change (step 1). This may include scanning societal changes and informing villagers accordingly and organizing meetings to present information about societal change, involving external 'neutral' partners. For step 2 – understanding and agreeing on the cause–effect relationship – support could involve external research institutions, considered neutral, to provide analyses on the causality between an innovation and any harmful societal changes. The support may include the presentation of information from these different sources and organizing meetings to facilitate a discussion interpreting whether or not there is a link. Subsequently the progression to internal regulation could be facilitated by enabling the community to weigh the positive and negative outcomes of the innovation and accept any trade-offs (step 3). This could be by presenting information about the costs and benefits of the innovation, so that villagers themselves can balance and judge according to their set of norms. If there is not a trade-off settlement, support could be in form of mediation and encouraging innovators to behave responsibly (step 4). If there is ambiguity in the attitudes and behaviour of innovators, external support could challenge the innovators to take a position over whether they acknowledge responsibility or not, and encourage the innovators to behave altruistically and call them to account. If external regulation is inevitable, external support could be in sorting out and facilitating juridical procedures, mobilizing existing institutions or encouraging institutional change/reform (step 5).

A last consideration for promoting internal regulation is the challenge to develop micro-level responses that are context specific. In terms of the Vietnamese cases, these could manifest in an 'independent' policy-making and implementation entity at the village level. Such an entity within the village administration would be able to analyse and understand the innovation outcomes, their societal consequences and locals' perceptions. The credibility of facilitating the societal process at the village level will depend on its autonomy and ability to interpret the innovation manifestations, societal outcomes and perceptions and to autonomously develop and implement context-specific innovation policy measures. Moreover, context-specific policy measures should be monitored on an ongoing basis, by involving the societal process model for instance, so as to respond quickly to emerging issues arising from these types of inclusive innovation. In conclusion, promoting internal regulation is about monitoring the quality of the process rather than measuring the outcomes.

7. Concluding remarks

This paper started out by noting, uncontroversially, that firm-level innovation may have negative societal impacts, and that this necessitates external regulation. What is less well established, however, is whether and how internal regulation, by firms themselves, can limit the negative externalities of innovative activities. This may be especially relevant in developing countries where institutional features that support external regulation are often lacking, and particularly so for inclusive innovations that derive from lower income communities where the writ of formal institutions runs least. Focusing on the case of inclusive innovation in Vietnamese craft villages, we found that cluster-level, as opposed to firm-level, innovation is a notable manifestation and also that the innovation generated in this context can have negative externalities. We explored to what extent internal regulation did or not limit these. We found evidence of innovators who acknowledged responsibility for the pollution they created and acted by introducing cleaner technology. By comparing a set of cases, we conceptualized and modelled inclusive innovation and regulation of its externalities as a 'societal process'. In essence, the model describes a series of internal regulation steps at the micro-level: community members who benefit from the craft village innovations, perceive and respond to the negative externalities; through various social interactions they may agree on what is acceptable and what is not, or force innovators within the cluster to acknowledge responsibility, thus concluding an internal regulation arrangement.

With regard to current ideas on internal regulation, CSR and sustainable business approaches typically take the form of a pre-defined strategy within a firm including targets set and measured, audited and owned by external experts. The 'societal process' model of inclusive innovation described in this paper is different in the sense that the societal process is an unpredictable emergent process implicitly owned by the community members. Consequently, acknowledging responsibility for negative innovation externalities in the societal process model is not a strategic decision taken at the firm level, but the result of emergent innovation consequences, involving close interactions and informal coordination among actors at the cluster level. Local normative frameworks apply in assessing and valuing the outcomes. The generalizability of the societal process model to other locations in Vietnam is supported by evidence of numerous other craft villages with very similar characteristics of informally organized small producers' clusters, which have been an essential part of Vietnam's rural economy and society for many centuries. Moreover, economic dynamics accompanied by harmful environmental and social consequences in the context of poor producers' clusters are common in many developing countries (Blackman 2006, de Oliveira 2008).

The societal process described here therefore could complement the 'projectified' approach of internal regulation, in particular on the emerging societal conflicts of firms' operations involving many visible and invisible stakeholders in informal contexts, often a problem in developing countries. Although large corporations may have a CSR strategy in place, including compliance to a pre-defined set of outcome indicators, societal conflict arises when (unexpected) long-term impacts surface. Local communities apply their local normative framework in assessing emerging insights and perceptions.

Whether the societal process model described here also applies to other developing country settings remains a topic for future research. We suspect that it may be valuable and perhaps even applicable, since the process as described contains the typical elements of inclusive innovation. It also includes the local normative dimension in valuing of externalities, which is less commonly applied in current expert-based policy and research approaches.

Finally, one remaining difficulty of involving local normative frameworks concerns an ethical issue: if small producers damage their health over the long term by achieving short-term income goals and public policy research is aware of it, then promoting the involvement of local normative frameworks is ethically debatable. Although the levels of acceptability may vary from one village to another, long-term development goals may not be compromised. Policies need to be different precisely to achieve similar societal goals in different settings. This is still a difficulty in the model and a challenge for further research into internal regulation.

Notes

1. A craft village is understood to be a rural village where at least 50% of households engage in off-farm activities and at least 30% of the village's income is derived from such activities. A traditional craft is seen as one that has existed for at least 50 years, reflects Vietnamese cultural identity and is practised by artisans in the village.
2. The research was part of a larger Dutch research project on responsible innovation in developing countries funded by the Netherlands Organization for Scientific Research (NWO) from 2009 to 2012.
3. Kaplinsky and Morris (2001) identified various types of innovation: (i) process innovation aiming at improving the efficiency of transforming inputs into outputs; (ii) product innovation leading to better quality, lower price and/or more differentiated products; (iii) business practice innovation implying new ways to organize business and attract new clients; (iv) functional innovations – assuming responsibility for new activities in the value chain, such as design, marketing and logistics and (v) inter-chain innovations moving to new and profitable chains.

References

Alkire, S. 2007. "Choosing Dimensions: The Capability Approach and Multidimensional Poverty." Chronic Poverty Research Centre Working Paper No. 88. http://dx.doi.org/10.2139/ssrn.1646411

Aubert, J.-E. 2005. "Promoting Innovation in Developing Countries: A Conceptual Framework." Policy Research Working Paper No. 3554. Washington: World Bank Publications.

Baumol, W. 1990. "Entrepreneurship: Productive, Unproductive and Destructive." *Journal of Political Economy* 98 (5): 893–921.

Blackman, A. ed. 2006. *Small Firms and the Environment in Developing Countries*. Washington, DC: Resources for the Future.

Bowden, H. R. 1953. *Social Responsibilities of the Businessman*. New York, NY: Harper.

Caniëls, Marjolein, and Henny Romijn. 2007. "Does Innovation Matter for LDCs? Discussion and New Agenda." Paper presented at the Centre for Advanced Study (CAS) Workshop 'Innovation in Firms', Oslo, Norway, October 30–November 1.

Cioffi, J. 2000. "Governing Globalisation? The State, Law, and Structural Change in Corporate Governance." *Journal of Law and Society* 27 (4): 572–600.

Cling, J. P., M. Razafindrakoto, and F. Roubaus. 2011. "The Informal Sector in Vietnam." Report of the International Labour Organization. Accessed December 15, 2013. http://www.ilo.org/wcmsp5/groups/public/—asia/—ro-bangkok/—ilo-hanoi/documents/publication/wcms_171370.pdf

Collier, P. 1998. "The Role of the State in Economic Development: Cross-regional Experiences." *Journal of African Economies* 7 (suppl. 2): 38–76.

Cozzens, S., and S. Kaplinsky. 2009. "Innovation, Poverty and Inequality: Cause, Coincidence of Co-evolution." In Handbook of *Innovation Systems and Developing Countries – Building Domestic Capabilities in a Global Setting*, edited by B.-Å. Lundvall, K. Joseph, C. Chaminade, and J. Vang, 57–92. Cheltenham: Edward Elgar.

Desai, S., Z. J. Acs, and U. Weitzel. 2013. "A Model of Destructive Entrepreneurship: Insight for Conflict and Postconflict Recovery." *Journal of Conflict Resolution* 57 (1): 20–40.

Dosi, Giovanni. 1988. "The Nature of the Innovation Process." In *Technical Change and Economic Theory*, edited by G. Dosi, C. Freeman, R. Nelson, G. Silverberg, and L. Soete, 221–238. London: Pinter Publishers.

Dutz, M. A. ed. 2007. *Unleashing India's Innovation: Toward Sustainable and Inclusive Growth.* Washington, DC: World Bank.

Elkington, J. 1999. *Cannibals with Forks, the Triple Bottom Line of the 21st Century Business.* Oxford: Capstone.

Fagerberg, J., D. C. Mowery, and R. R. Nelson. eds. 2005. *The Oxford Handbook of Innovation.* Oxford: Oxford University Press.

Ferreira, F., and M. Ravallion. 2009. "Poverty and Inequality: The Global Context." In *The Oxford Handbook of Economic Inequality*, edited by W. Salverda, B. Nolan, and T. Smeeding, 599–638. Oxford: Oxford University Press.

Frederick, W. 1960. "The Growing Concern Over Business Responsibility." *California Management Review* 2 (4): 54–61.

Freeman, R. E. 1984. *Strategic Management: A Stakeholder Approach.* Englewood Cliffs, NJ: Prentice Hall.

Gebreeyesus, M. 2011. "Innovation and Microenterprise Growth in Ethiopia." In *Entrepreneurship Innovation and Economic Development*, edited by A. Szirmai, W. Naudé, and M. Goedhuys, 122–146. Oxford: Oxford University Press.

Gellynck, X., B. Kühne, and R. D. Weaver. 2011. "Innovation Capacity of Food Chains: A Novel Approach." *International Journal of Innovation and Regional Development* 3 (2): 99–112.

George, G., A. McGahan, and J. Prabhu. 2012. "Innovation for Inclusive Growth: Towards a Theoretical Framework and a Research Agenda." *Journal of Management Studies* 49 (4): 661–683.

Gladwell, Malcolm. 2000. *The Tipping Point: How Little Things can make a Big Difference.* Boston, MA: Back Bay Books.

Glaser, B. G., and A. L. Strauss. 1967. *The Discovery of Grounded Theory: Strategies for Qualitative Research.* Chicago: Aldine.

Gries, T., and W. A. Naudé. 2011. "Entrepreneurship and Human Development: A Capability Approach." *Journal of Public Economics* 95 (3): 216–224.

Hardin, G. 1968. "The Tragedy of the Commons." *Science* 162 (3859): 1243–1248. doi:10.1126/science. 162.3859.1243.

Hart, S. 2007. *Capitalism at the Crossroads – Aligning Business, Earth and Humanity.* 2nd ed. Upper Saddle River, NJ: Wharton School Publishing.

Hart, S. M. 2009. "Self-regulation, Corporate Social Responsibility, and the Business Case: Do they Work in Achieving Workplace. Equality and Safety?" *Journal of Business Ethics* 92 (4): 585–600. doi:10.1007/s10551-009-0174-1.

Howlett, M., and M. Ramesh. 1995. *Studying Public Policy: Policy Cycles and Policy Subsystems.* New York: Oxford University Press.

IMF. 2008. *World Economic Outlook Database.* Washington, DC: International Monetary Fund.

Kaplinsky, R., and M. Morris. 2001. *A Handbook for Value Chain Research.* Brighton: Institute of Development Studies (IDS), University of Sussex.

Kline, S. J., and N. Rosenberg. 1986. "An Overview of Innovation." In *The Positive Sum Strategy: Harnessing Technology for Economic Growth*, edited by R. Landau and N. Rosenberg, 275–305. Washington, DC: National Academies Press.

Konstadakopulos, D. 2005. "From Public Loudspeakers to the Internet: The Adoption of Information and Communication Technologies (ICTs) by Small-Enterprise Clusters in Vietnam." *Information Technologies and International Development* 2 (4): 21–39.

Léger, A., and S. Swaminathan. 2007. "Innovation Theories: Relevance and Implications for Developing Country Innovation." Discussion Papers 743. Berlin: Deutsches Institut für Wirtschaftsforschung.

Levi-Faur, D. 2005. "The Global Diffusion of Regulatory Capitalism." *Annals of the American Academy of Political and Social Science* 598: 12–32.

London, T. 2007. "A Base-of-the-Pyramid Perspective on Poverty Alleviation." Growing Inclusive Markets Working Paper Series. Washington, DC: United Nations Development Program.

Lundvall, Bengt-Åke. 1992. *National Systems of Innovation: Towards a Theory of Innovation and Interactive Learning.* London: Pinter Publishers.

Nelson, R., and S. Winter. 1977. "In Search of a Useful Theory of Innovation." *Research Policy* 6 (1): 36–76.

Nguyen, K. Q., V. T. Tran, and V. L. Le. 2003. "Project Vie/00/018/08: Assessing Participatory Rural Environmental Management in the Craft Villages (Cat Que Commune, Hoai Duc Distrit, Ha Tay Province)." Report of the Vietnam Agricultural Science Institute, Hanoi.

Nill, J., and R. Kemp. 2009. "Evolutionary Approaches for Sustainable Innovation Policies: From Niche to Paradigm?" *Research Policy Special Issue: Emerging Challenges for Science, Technology and Innovation Policy Research* 38 (4): 668–680.

Nutley, S., H. Davies, and P. Smith. 2000. *What Works?: Evidence-Based Policy and Practice in Public Services*. Bristol: The Policy Press.

OECD. 2005. *The Measurement of Scientific and Technological Activities – Proposed Guidelines for Collecting and Interpreting Technological Innovation Data*. Paris: Organization for Economic Co-operation and Development (OECD), Eurostat.

OECD. 2012. *Innovation for Development – A discussion of the Issues and an Overview of Work of the OECD Directorate for Science, Technology and Industry*. Paris: Organisation for Economic Co-operation and Development (OECD). Accessed January 14, 2014. http://www.oecd.org/sti/inno/50586251.pdf

de Oliveira, J. A. P. ed. 2008. *Upgrading Clusters and Small Enterprises in Developing Countries: Environmental, Labor, Innovation and Social Issues*. Farnham: Ashgate.

Ostrom, E., J. Burger, Ch. Field, R. Norgaard, and D. Policansky. 1999. "Revisiting the Commons: Local Lessons, Global Challenges." *Science* 284 (5412): 278–282.

Palzer, C., and A. Scheuer. 2003. "Self-Regulation, Co-Regulation, Public Regulation." In *Promote or Protect? Perspectives on Media Literacy and Media Regulations*, edited by U. Carlsson and C. von Feilitzen, 165–178. Göteborg: The UNESCO International Clearinghouse on Children and Violence on the Screen.

Parker, C. 2002. *The Open Corporation: Effective Self-regulation and Democracy*. Cambridge: Cambridge University Press.

Radjou, N., J. Prabhu, and S. Ahuja. 2012. *Jugaad Innovation: Think Frugal, Be Flexible, Generate Breakthrough Growth*. San Francisco, CA: Jossey-Bass.

Rand, J., and N. Torm. 2012. "The Benefits of Formalization: Evidence from Vietnamese Manufacturing SMEs." *World Development* 40 (5): 983–998.

Rutten, R., and F. Boekema. 2007. *The Learning Region: Foundations, State of the Art, Future*. Cheltenham: Edward Elgar.

Sanders, M., and U. Weitzel. 2013. "Misallocation of Entrepreneurial Talent in Postconflict Environments." *Journal of Conflict Resolution* 57 (1): 41–64.

Sanderson, I. 2002. "Evaluation, Policy Learning and Evidence-Based Policy Making." *Public Administration* 80 (1): 1–22.

Schmitz, H. 1999. "Collective Efficiency and Increasing Returns." *Cambridge Journal of Economics* 23 (4): 465–483.

Sen, A. 1999. *Development as Freedom*. Oxford: Oxford University Press.

Soete, L. 2012. "Maastricht Reflections on Innovation." UNU-MERIT Working Paper no. 2012–001.

Soman, D., J. G. Stein, and J. Wong. eds. 2014. *Innovating for the Global South: Towards an Inclusive Innovation Agenda*. Toronto, ON: University of Toronto Press.

Szirmai, A. 2008. "Explaining Success and Failure in Development." Working Paper 2008–013. Maastricht: UNU-MERIT.

Szirmai, A., W. Naudé, and M. Goedhuys. 2011. *Entrepreneurship, Innovation, and Economic Development*. Oxford: Oxford University Press.

Utz, A., and C. Dahlman. 2007. "Promoting Inclusive Innovation." In *Unleashing India's Innovation: Toward Sustainable and Inclusive Growth*, edited by M. Dutz, 105–128. Washington, DC: The World Bank.

Van Dijk, M. P., and H. Sandee. 2002. *Innovation and Small Enterprises in the Third World*. Cheltenham: Edward Elgar.

Voeten, J., J. de Haan, and G. de Groot. 2011. "Is That Innovation? Assessing Examples of Revitalized Economic Dynamics among Clusters of Small Producers in Northern Vietnam." In *Entrepreneurship, Innovation, and Economic Development*, edited by A. Szirmai, W. Naudé, and M. Goedhuys, 96–121. Oxford: Oxford University Press.

Voeten, J., N. Roome, G. de Groot, and J. de Haan. 2012. "Resolving Environmental and Social Conflicts – Responsible Innovation in Small Producers' Clusters in Northern Vietnam." In *A stakeholder Approach* to *Corporate Social Responsibility: Pressures, Conflicts, Reconciliation*, edited by A. Lindgreen, Ph. Kotler, J. Vanhamme, and F. Maon, 243–261. Aldershot: Gower.

Watts, D., and S. Strogatz. 1998. "Collective Dynamics of 'Small World' Networks." *Nature* 393 (6684): 440–442.

Wolf, S. 2007. "Encouraging Innovation for Productivity Growth in Africa." Work in Progress Series 54, African Trade Policy Centre (ATPC), UNECA ATPC, Addis Ababa.

World Bank. 2008. *Growth Report: Strategies for Sustained Growth and Inclusive Development.* Washington, DC: World Bank Growth and Development Commission.

World Bank. 2012. "Vietnam development report 2012, Market Economy for a Middle-Income Vietnam." Joint Donor Report to the Vietnam Consultative Group Meeting, December 6, 2011.

Zeschky, M., B. Widenmayer, and G. Oliver. 2011. "Frugal Innovation in Emerging Markets." *Research-Technology Management* 54 (4): 38–45.

Nurturing user–producer interaction: inclusive innovation flows in a low-income mobile phone market

Christopher Foster[a] and Richard Heeks[b]

[a]Oxford Internet Institute, University of Oxford, Oxford, UK; [b]Centre for Development Informatics, IDPM, University of Manchester, Manchester, UK

Understandings of inclusive innovation in developing country low-income markets have typically taken one of two perspectives. On the one hand, a business perspective on the role of top-down, strategic innovation from larger-firm actors. And on the other hand, a more developmental perspective that highlights the role localized practices play in making new goods and services applicable to local needs. Both are demonstrably important to successful inclusive innovation but, to date, there has been little analysis of the link between these two perspectives. The goal of this paper is to explore the interaction between top-down and localized elements of innovation, and to provide an understanding of the conditions by which these two perspectives might be complementary. Drawing on the case of the mobile phone sector in Kenya, and adapting Lundvall's concept of user–producer interaction, a conceptual model to understand such innovation flows is outlined. This highlights the centrality of operational links between producers and users which serve as a medium for interactive learning.

1. Introduction

There is a growth of interest in the idea of inclusive innovation – understood particularly as innovation which provides benefits for low-income groups in developing countries (Altenburg 2009; Cozzens and Kaplinsky 2009; Foster and Heeks 2013a).

Two main directions can be discerned from literature where such inclusivity has been discussed. Management literature, particularly revolving around 'base-of-the-pyramid' markets (Hart and London 2005; Prahalad 2009), has positioned innovation for low-income communities as predominantly a top-down, strategic and firm-led exercise, where innovations are refined to have efficacy in these markets. Inclusion is thus a process of managing and directing innovation undertaken by those external to the context of consumption. In contrast, a second direction has emerged which views inclusive innovation from a more developmental perspective, and focuses on more diverse and micro-level innovation activities (Cozzens and Sutz 2012; Singh, Gupta, and Mondal 2011; Utz and Dahlman 2007). In this case, inclusion is a more emergent process undertaken by those within and around localized contexts.

To date in the literature there has been a division between these two approaches to inclusive innovation in low-income markets: one arising from the business discourse of management of innovation in emerging markets, the other more influenced by development studies and approaches to supporting livelihoods. Here we argue that better links between these two perspectives are important in more clearly understanding how innovation can be more inclusive:

For firms innovating for low-income groups: more complete perspectives on localized innovation processes provide insight for larger firms into more effective design and scaling of appropriate innovations, promoting both profitability and inclusivity. How such firms understand and link to these rich localized processes should be a subject of core interest, since it can be central for success in such markets (Foster and Heeks 2013a).

For actors working with localized innovation processes: local or grassroots innovation is typically seen as isolated from wider flows of innovation, and restricted by local resource and capacity constraints. This paper argues for a more relational perspective, where external pressures and knowledge flows are crucial in shaping the actions of local innovators.

The paper is presented as follows. In the next section, these two directions related to inclusive innovation are explored more thoroughly, and some suggestions from literature are discussed on how best to understand the link between them. It is argued that interactive learning models of systems of innovation provide a potential basis for an analytical connection: specifically, a revival of Lundvall's concept of user–producer interaction (Lundvall 1988, 1992a). User–producer interaction highlights the centrality of relations between innovation producers and users; those relations serving as a medium of interactive learning. However, given the specificities of the actors and divergent processes of innovation in low-income markets, this model needs to be revisited in light of empirical work, refining the conceptualization to fit those specificities.

To provide this empirical insight, the paper next draws on the case of the mobile phone sector in Kenya which has developed through an intersection of both top-down and localized innovation. In this case, user–producer interactions are best understood by examining the indirect elements of managerial and technical control between users and producers, and the configuration of user–producer relations.

In sum, this paper extends current literature in two ways. Conceptually, the paper revives and extends the notion of user–producer interactions. It shows how this can provide a new basis for understanding the links between top-down and localized processes of inclusive innovation. Practically, this conceptual approach exposes key issues – both for large firms and those involved with localized innovation – that are critical to successful inclusive innovation, but which have to date not been dealt with substantively.

2. Innovation and inclusivity: two directions

2.1. *Base-of-the-pyramid and innovation*

Work around base-of-the-pyramid (BoP) markets predominantly looks at successful strategies led by large firms which see low-income groups as untapped markets (Hart and London 2005; Prahalad 2009). Their innovations are inclusive in the sense of consumption; inclusivity arising from adoption and use of goods and services by the poor who have traditionally been excluded from such innovations (Heeks et al. 2013). In this work, innovation of relevant products for low-income groups is seen to centre around adaptations which fit the unique cultural, financial and social needs of such groups (Prahalad 2006).

Successful BoP ventures are seen to require a connection to local consumers – understanding their context during design to allow those adaptations, and using suitable marketing and retail supply chains (including local entrepreneurs) in order to deliver the new goods or services to market (Hart and Christensen 2002; London and Hart 2004). This connection sometimes goes further, in joint 'co-creation' activities in the early stages of the innovation cycle that draw in local capabilities (London, Anupindi, and Sheth 2010; Simanis and Hart 2009).

Yet, there are still significant gaps in base-of-the-pyramid conceptions of local innovators because these adopt the worldview of the lead firm. Thus, BoP literature has been critiqued for viewing any local innovation inputs solely through an instrumental lens that values it principally in terms of bottom-line contribution (Arora and Romijn 2013). The primary focus from this business-and-management-derived literature is the lead firm and its management strategy. This literature therefore tends to provide an impoverished view of local inputs to inclusive innovation that simplifies their breadth and complexity, and underplays their significance.

These conceptual weaknesses undermine practical relevance. With limited recognition of the full nature, richness and importance of localized innovation, there is little guidance for lead firms on how to recognize, analyse and integrate that innovation. This is particularly an issue for innovation at scale: when firms interact with and nurture an increasing number and diversity of actors, management becomes more complex (Anderson and Kupp 2008; Foster and Heeks 2013b).

In essence, the base-of-the-pyramid perspective – for all its 'co-production' rhetoric – treats innovation as a top-down, strategic and firm-managed activity once early stages have been completed. This is a view out-of-synch with the realities of inclusive innovation; particularly when scaled.

2.2. *Localized innovation*

A separate strand of literature – influenced more by development studies than by business and management – has been looking at the more incremental and adaptive innovation activities that happen within and around the local contexts of consumption in developing countries (Cozzens and Sutz 2012; Singh, Gupta, and Mondal 2011; Utz and Dahlman 2007). Innovation is seen as inclusive if it has a positive impact on the livelihoods of the poor and, to so some degree, if members of low-income communities are involved in its development (Heeks et al. 2013).

Alongside being called 'inclusive', such innovation has been given many other labels, each with its own nuance: indigenous, pro-poor, local, grassroots, informal, frugal. As an overall, these cover a range of incremental local practices – adaptation, appropriation, configuration, domestication – undertaken by a range of local actors – micro-entrepreneurs, community members, activists – previously underplayed in innovation studies (Foster and Heeks 2013a). In these contexts, innovation is articulated as emerging in the unique conditions, practices and constraints of low-income settings where communities use their knowledge to solve problems and share solutions relevant to their local needs and settings.

The literature cited above has shown these localized actions to be essential to the effective adoption and use of innovation, and this has broader impact. While it may not necessarily link directly into wider economic growth, such activity can be essential at a micro-level by allowing citizens to build employment, income, resilience and position in society (Arocena and Sutz 2000; Cozzens and Kaplinsky 2009; Lundvall 2011). These are all vital to ensuring livelihoods, and they identify localized processes of innovation as being of significant developmental importance.

This literature has generally focussed on the practices of localized innovation. There has been some link acknowledged between such activity and wider context: e.g. institutional support for local emergence of innovations (Berdegué 2005; Utz and Dahlman 2007), or the connection of grassroots innovators into external value chains (Kaplinsky et al. 2009; Kraemer-Mbula and Wamae 2010). But such work on linking has been sporadic, dispersed in its focus, and limited in empirical foundation.

This is surprising given the growing incursion of large-firm-led goods and services into BoP markets; which at the least is influencing, and at the most orientating local innovation practice – in agriculture, in manufacturing, in telecommunications, etc. Yet, just as with the BoP literature, there is this disconnect. Further research is needed to help understand and instantiate the wider influences that increasingly connect to and affect localized innovation.

2.3. *Dangers of the disconnect*

One can see this disconnect between approaches as more than a conceptual shortcoming arising from cross-disciplinary detachment. It is also marginalizing real-world cross-level interactions, and thus reducing the availability of practical guidance.

As noted above, firms looking to focus on low-income markets need a clear basis for understanding and nurturing localized innovation processes. Such processes will help them produce appropriate products, and can be amplified in order to allow those products to scale more rapidly. For localized innovation, it is important to understand the local context, but not to the exclusion of all other variables. Local entrepreneurs and innovators, and those who facilitate them through direct support or indirect policy, are in danger of missing the bigger picture. With a cross-level relational analysis, that bigger picture can be better provided.

In this context, the goal of this paper is to answer the following question:

How do we conceptually link the top-down and localized components of inclusive innovation?

2.4. *Connecting top-down and localized innovation via systems approaches*

It is suggested here that approaches based upon adapted systems of innovation models, and more specifically the use of Lundvall's concept of user–producer interaction (Lundvall 1988, 1992a), can build an understanding of interaction and flows between top-down and localized innovation.

Systems of innovation approaches are now firmly established as providing an evidentially supported holistic understanding of innovation, and as a tool in policy making, replacing 'linear model' approaches (Edquist 1997; Freeman 1995; Lundvall 1992b). They centralize the notion of innovation as a driver of development and offer a systematic understanding of the interactive behaviour of a number of actors – firms, support organizations, research bodies, policy makers and implementers – who contribute to innovation (Freeman 1995). In developing country settings, these approaches have mainly been used to analyse large, formal structures of innovation at national level such as interaction between universities, research, policy and support agencies (Lundvall and Intarakumnerd 2006; Lundvall, Joseph, and Chaminade 2009). However, even where innovation activities and institutions are less formal and well defined, systems approaches have been used to examine the ways of doing, using and interacting (DUI) related to innovation (Lundvall et al. 2009). Such perspectives define innovation as emerging in the 'wider' everyday processes of interactive learning by multiple system actors rather than restricting themselves to 'narrower' definitions which only encompass formal institutional interactions (Lundvall et al. 2009).

By definition, a DUI perspective on innovation has a particular interest in the varieties of interaction that take place between all actors, since these are seen to ultimately determine the nature and outcome of innovation. Lundvall's work on user–producer interactions provides one means to examine these connections in more detail (Lundvall 1988). Innovation is inherently an uncertain activity both on the supply side and demand side. On the supply side, producers are seen to need to understand user preferences and, hence, innovation requirements. On the demand side, users are seen to need to understand the utility of new innovations in order to make adoption decisions. User–producer interaction thus centralized the examination of the key relationships between

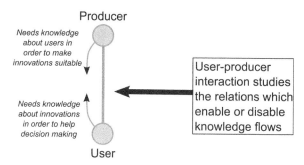

Figure 1.   User–producer interactions in innovation systems.
Source: Adapted from (Lundvall 1992b).

producers and users which determine how knowledge flows – and thus learning is built – between the two, as shown in Figure 1 (Lundvall 1988).

In a general sense, the use of DUI perspectives to examine sectoral innovation in developing countries has validated the importance of interaction and learning between actors; as highlighted in work on agricultural innovation systems (Clark 2002; Spielman, Ekboir, and Davis 2009; Sumberg 2005) and health innovation systems (Chataway et al. 2009; Mugabe 2005). It is argued that user–producer interaction concepts are vital to understanding these DUI processes around inclusive innovation, by analysing networks and relationships of actors, and the connection to flows of interactive learning (Nahuis, Moors, and Smits 2009). Further, these concepts can be particularly useful in considering the specificities surrounding inclusive innovation. In such scenarios, the gap of knowledge between user and producer is liable to be greater than for innovation addressing higher-income markets – producers know less about their consumers, consumers know less about new products. Closing this knowledge and learning gap and the consequent need for user–producer interaction is critical to inclusive innovation. By focusing on the way in which linkages enable or constrain knowledge and learning flows, the concept of user–producer interaction can thus be seen as one way to bridge the disconnect noted above between top-down and bottom-up innovation processes.

However, inclusive innovation systems focussing on lower-income users have been shown to be different in nature to the traditional innovation systems for which Lundvall's model was developed (Foster and Heeks 2013a). We will therefore need to modify that model, with Figure 2

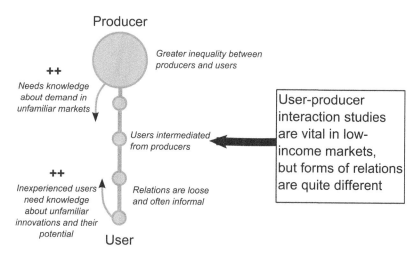

Figure 2.   Outline of user–producer interactions in low-income markets.

suggesting some elements of this. Users tend to be informal, heterogeneous and distributed. There may be a few powerful innovation producers linked to many relatively powerless low-income users. And relations between the two – because of the distance in terms of both geography and knowledge – will typically be intermediated often through a multitude of actors, with some of those intermediaries themselves being sources of knowledge, learning and innovation. But this is proposition, drawing on recent literature. To test the value of the model, empirical work is needed; first to clarify how to apply the user–producer interaction model to inclusive innovation; second to identify the practical implications of this conceptualisation.

3. Methodology

To apply the concept of user–producer interaction to inclusive innovation, empirical analysis is made of the mobile phone sector in Kenya, drawing on research focussing on low-income market delivery of mobile technologies and services. Worldwide, the mobile phone sector has seen rapid growth and is an ongoing source of both goods and services innovations. It was particularly chosen because it is the site of inclusive innovations matching the pattern described above: large-firm-led innovations which reach low-income users often at scale, but with local adaptations that result in unexpected uses and new behaviours in local contexts. Here we analyse two sub-sectors – mobile phone handset supply and mobile money services (cash transfers through mobile phone messaging) – which were purposively selected as having contrasting types of user–producer interaction (see the next section).

Work draws on semi-structured interviews undertaken as part of research on the mobile sector innovation system in Kenya in 2010 and 2011 involving in total 109 semi-structured interviews with innovation system actors: policy makers, handset producers, distributors and wholesalers, mobile money operators and agents, informal sellers and street hawkers and support organizations. Interviews were conducted with all principal policy makers, producers and distributors who would agree; and with a segmented sample of other stakeholders. Data gathering also included extensive document analysis, particularly relating to lead firms strategies of relevance to the two sub-sectors, and observational work of localized innovation practice. This therefore enabled a triangulation of both stakeholder perspectives and research methods (Neuman 2011).

Data from the three methods was digitized and then coded and analysed using NVivo 9, with a particular focus on issues and themes relating to actor interaction and learning. Next, this analysis of the networks in both cases is used to examine user–producer interactions and this is linked to the key genres of innovation occurring.

4. User–producer interactions

Our research finds that in these cases, at some stages, processes of top-down and localized innovation cohere well, and this leads to more inclusive innovation. At other times localized innovation is ignored, suppressed or constrained and this can lead to mismatch between the innovation interests of local actors and lead firm strategy. Below, empirical relations and outcomes are analysed taking each of the case studies in turn.

4.1. *Hierarchical interactions: mobile money*

The research reported here looks at the dominant mobile money service in Kenya; M-Pesa. The network of interactions for M-Pesa is shown in Figure 3. M-Pesa closely revolves around the lead

Figure 3.   Network of M-Pesa.
Source: Author fieldwork.

firm, mobile telecom operator Safaricom, which seeks to oversee all activities. Here we focus on person-to-person mobile transfer elements of the service which form the vast majority of low-income customers' M-Pesa transactions (Jack and Suri 2010; Stuart and Cohen 2011; World Bank 2011).

In this transfer network, operational responsibility is given to a number of actors which are separate from the lead firm. In particular there are a number of firms called 'agents' which run the core customer-facing element of mobile money services, engaging in cash deposit and withdrawal services for service users.[1] This occurs through a hierarchical arrangement where larger 'lead' agents sub-contract to smaller 'local' agents. It is the 'local' agents – small micro-enterprises – which provide the M-Pesa service to low-income customers. In addition, there is a strong quality monitoring presence, undertaken by several outsourced firms whose role is to visit agents to ensure that they are complying with rules and regulations as specified by the lead firm.

The M-Pesa service was found to be characteristic of hierarchical user–producer interactions where often 'user-producer relationships are characterized by strong dominance of producers' (Lundvall 1988, 356). In typical systems models, such one-sided relations have previously been seen to emerge out of financial and technical knowledge differentials between users and producers (Lundvall 1992a), but this is not the key method of control here. As shown in Figure 3, the innovation 'producer', Safaricom is only indirectly linked to low-income users through a number of intermediaries. Top-down direction is asserted through a number of elements of managerial and technical control including Safaricom rules, objects and threat of intermediaries being ejected from the network.

Where such direction is heavily exerted, this limits the extent to which consumers and particularly intermediaries can themselves adapt services according to local needs. This is illustrated by the case of Beatrice below:

Beatrice is an agent located in a small M-Pesa kiosk in the heart of a slum area 5 km from central Nairobi. One of the biggest problems that Beatrice faces in her agency related to the identification requirements in all M-Pesa deposits and withdrawals.[2] The problem is that many customers in this highly insecure area do not carry their ID card for fear of losing it. Other even-more marginal actors do not have, or cannot obtain an ID.[3]

Further, a common practice among such low-income groups is that younger family members carry out tasks for older working members of the family while they are busy working. However, according to M-Pesa rules, this would not be possible as the identification of the M-Pesa account and the family member would not match. As this is not permitted in the service, the transaction should be refused by an agent. Hence this rule limits this type of traditional activity.

To counter these dual problems around identification, Beatrice informally adapted the service to begin to allow trusted customers to transact without an ID, to better fit in with such customers who were highly common in her area. However when the M-Pesa monitoring firm sent an officer posing as a customer, she was seen doing this and caught.

For this breaking of the rules, Safaricom closed her kiosk for one month, nearly bankrupting the business. Now that she has reopened, she says that her customers are frustrated and frequently threatening when she refuses to transact without identification, but she cannot risk another forced closure.

In a hierarchical network, close attention to service compliance through monitoring and inspection means that certain local adaptations may be risky. In the example of Beatrice, the agent is trying to adapt the service to the needs and practices of her local users; but this hits regulatory constraints that have cascaded down the hierarchy.

Other hierarchical constraints are more subtle, but equally influential. One key limitation found was the service design that embedded assumptions of use, limiting growth of localized adaptation. In interviews, certain localized 'use change' service adaptations were found that depart from the predominant positioning and marketing of the service to users by Safaricom. Examples include:

- As one agent recounted 'when traders in the local area close at 6 or after, ... the banks are closed so they put their cash into M-Pesa!'. This method of storing money securely for short periods is a safety measure and used in some insecure areas, but this occurred only among certain entrepreneurs in very high risk areas due to the high commission costs incurred.[4]
- A number of informal stalls had signs that they accept M-Pesa as direct payment, thus simplifying the need to hold cash on both customer and business sides. However, when asked, stallholders stated that such payments were no longer accepted, or only for bulk purchases due to the delays that were common in the network, and the confusion that this caused for stallholders.
- Using M-Pesa as a way to build very small levels of savings, particularly among slum dwellers is common. However, this seemingly important approach to saving had only been adopted by a few local credit and micro-finance associations, due to the costs and account limitations.

As highlighted, 'use change' adaptations were found in individual locations, but they hit service design barriers – around high commission costs, technical limitation of the service, or service rules.

Thus, there are a variety of ways that localized innovations are constrained or otherwise shaped by top-down flows. As shown in these examples, sometimes this comes through more obvious activities such as top-down rule setting and policing which more explicitly constrains behaviour. However, more 'tacit' top-down elements such as service barriers also play a key role, and a range of different aspects – training, rules and regulations, objects – were found to shape how localized innovation is undertaken in this service.

In this hierarchical network, learning on the demand side often links to how actors try to integrate and understand the features, rules and edicts that flow down from the producer. As highlighted by one agent's discussions of his interactions, these tend to be one-way flows that rarely provide room for feedback from the local level:

We get lots of SMS from Safaricom – normally advice and about network problems .... There are sometimes meeting for agents. I went to one a month ago. Last time they were training us about M-Kesho [*a new element of the M-Pesa service*].

This learning may crowd out localized innovation yet, often, these local adaptations and domes-tications are crucial in making the service more relevant to users. By constraining localized inno-vation, the two examples outlined above – limitations to adaptation around ID rules and 'use changes' – directly reduced the utility and adoption of the M-Pesa service, and consequently reduced its inclusivity.

From a user–producer perspective, if producers are appropriately connected to users they may be able to identify such local needs and adaptations, and then modify either top-down constraints or the core innovations themselves to better fit the local contexts. While there was some evidence from the case study literature on M-Pesa that user–producer interaction had previously been less hierarchical, particularly during the earlier trial periods (Hughes and Lonie 2007), there was a lack of evidence during this study that producers were seeking to support localized innovation. Indeed this was to the frustration of intermediary dealers:

> … we don't have much say with them [*Safaricom*] … .dealers are feeling demoralised. There is room for someone to come up with an alternative and maybe dealers would take them up.

This likely relates to the lack of direct linkage between producer and users, and the uneven size and power of these actors which precludes a clear flow of interactive learning back to producers even were there to be some linkage.

4.2. *Market interactions: mobile handsets*

While mobile handsets are sold through networks linked to formally designated shops in large towns generally focussed towards more affluent users (right-hand side in Figure 4), lower-income users tend to purchase phones through more complex alternative channels (left-hand side in Figure 4).

The research reported here investigated the latter – growing 'informal' channels that link to sellers in trading areas, markets and kiosks. In Kenya, such sellers are independent micro-enter-prises, who link to mobile handset suppliers and operators through intermediaries such as phone wholesalers and distributors. This channel also involves a diverse set of handsets including both 'branded phones' (multinational handset brands), 'grey-market' (branded handsets imported unofficially, often without paying tax), second-hand phones, and so-called 'China phones' (emer-gent Chinese firms producing low-cost phones).

Originally, these informal channels were exclusively used to sell grey-market and second-hand phones, as a way of providing cheaper goods for lower-income users. But, more recently, international firms, increasingly aware of the need to focus on lower-income groups, have them-selves integrated into these channels using new 'dedicated distributors' for their higher-quality phones.

Like the M-Pesa case, the handset sub-sector is characteristic of user–producer interactions that are (dis)connected through a number of intermediaries. Indeed, as shown in Figure 4, in this case this disconnection is more marked, with a greater number of intermediaries and/or with handset producers primarily located outside Kenya.

This fits closely with the pattern of market-based user–producer interactions outlined by Lundvall, when social relations are minimal (at least for producers), and where 'producers would have difficulties in observing new user needs, and users would lack qualitative information on the characteristics of the new products' (Lundvall 1992a, 50). In the informal mobile handset channels this was found to occur because the network of links from producers to users was not only marketized but also quite complex, interchangeable and heavily intermediated.

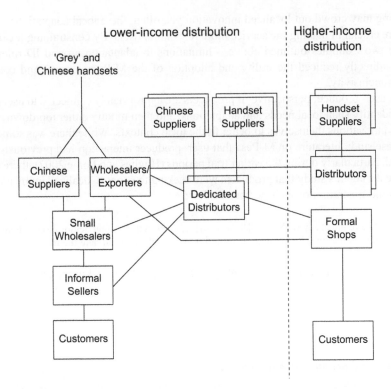

Figure 4.   Networks in mobile handset case.
Source: Author fieldwork.

As highlighted in the original conception of user–producer interaction, this has a detrimental effect both on users' ability to understand and appropriate select technologies, and on producers' ability to adapt goods and services to users.

For users, disconnected user–producer interactions meant that local demand-side actors struggled to identify appropriate goods for users. This is highlighted in the case of Evans below.

Evans, a handset seller, was interviewed in the slum area surveyed. He owned two small kiosks, one in this slum and another in his rural hometown. Originally he sold electrical parts for nearby 'Jua Kali' (informal SME) producers, but he diversified into mobile handset selling which was now his main income generator.

To get supply he would go to a wholesaler located in the central districts of Nairobi around 10 km away. In describing his interactions with this supplier, Evans outlined how he had run into a number of problems when he began, connected to his predominant focus on selling cheaper Chinese and imported phones to low-income users.

I sold China phones but there were problems with faults and warranties … It was costing me time and effort. I no longer stock!

His principal problem related to supply quality and this was exacerbated by not being closely connected to wholesalers. With a comparatively low turnover in stock due to his location, he had little ability to build thick relationships with wholesalers and build knowledge of trustworthy suppliers of handsets. This poor link also had a secondary effect in that it reduced his ability to get wholesaler credit that could aid growth.

I go to just one, and pay in cash. We are far away from the centre and not regular enough to know them or build credit with them …

As highlighted with Evans, a lack of relations to producers and informal relations to other intermediaries were to the detriment of understanding the quality of goods. With a lack of clear links to producers, learning and innovation in the handset sub-sector mainly focused on intermediaries' survival in, and adaptation for local markets – including tactics to diversify stocks or otherwise ensure viability of their business – rather than specific adaptations of the technology itself for or by users.

From the producer side, with a lack of close connection there was little consideration, or amplification, of specific adaptations connected to these markets. For instance, informal mobile sellers in low-income areas are marked by widespread socio-technical adaptations – in the forms of selling and supply, in the informal networks and processes of trade and repair; and in specific elements of local use such as recharging tactics and money saving through multiple-sim use. But any diffusion of these localized innovations mainly occurred through local micro-entrepreneurs imitating each other, rather than in a clear feedback of knowledge and ideas to lead firms. As a result, lead firms continued to produce handset models that were poorly matched to local needs and/or distributed in inappropriate ways, reducing the inclusivity of this technology in terms of its adoption and use by low-income consumers.

Generally, therefore, in the handset sub-sector marketized relationships *and* high levels of intermediation have led to a lack of relations between users and producers, and this has been detrimental to both. However, there is some evidence that recent changes might help improve user–producer relations. The growth in 'dedicated distribution' to lower-income consumers set up by large handset firms (see the left-hand side of Figure 4) is helping to develop the connection to less formal actors. Accounts from handset firms involved in this activity indicate that there is an increasing flow of marketing, data and even knowledge between themselves and users. These improved flows between low-income users and producers can be linked to recent initiatives around nurturing distribution actors and deliberately seeking to develop devices better adapted for low-income users. For instance, one large supplier has sought to increase the extent of face-to-face interaction within its dedicated distribution channel, to build social rather than purely marketized relations. In parallel, they have been able to make technical adaptations – with local language options, more appropriate hardware specifications, and even a rural-focussed application being created for their phones. The evidence is that these innovations have been shaped by better flows – both direct data and tacit knowledge – from low-income users.

5. Discussion

For inclusive innovation systems addressing low-income consumers, given a DUI approach, the general nature of user–producer interactions has been examined in terms of the operational networks around these innovations. These elements define the nature of user–producer relationships and consequently provide insights into modes of learning and risks. These are outlined in more detail below.

5.1. *Characterizing user–producer interaction*

In the Kenyan mobile sector, as predicted by the literature review, user–producer relationships are characterized as being rather different to those originally conceived by Lundvall. In both cases, we can chart those relationships as starting with a few large producers associated with an innovation, then moving down through a set of mid-size intermediaries, to local intermediaries, to users. Also in line with the literature study, evidence suggests that user–producer interactions are vital – of course in the resource flow of core goods and services – but also in knowledge flows between the two which underpin effective selection and adaptation of innovations; that adaptation being so necessary in markets where low-income users often have unique and localized demands. Next, we examine in more detail how best to define and examine user–producer interactions in these low-income DUI systems.

First, on the demand-side of innovation, in addition to users, local intermediaries will be a key actor, whose linkages and learning are crucial. Many of the locally innovative activities and adaptations found in this case originally emerge from users themselves and/or from their interaction with demand-side intermediaries. But it is those demand-side intermediaries who are in a position to actively disseminate such innovations. This supports other work on intermediaries which is increasingly articulating their central role in refining and domesticating innovation on the one hand, and in brokering between users and producers on the other (Howells 2006; Stewart and Hyysalo 2008). Thus, rather than conceiving user–producer relations in direct terms, it may be more appropriate to understand them in terms of the skills and activities of locally embedded intermediaries on the demand side. This links closely to Lundvall's discussions around *capability on the demand side* in user–producer interactions and the ability of users or other demand-side actors to actively voice their own needs and ideas, and their ability to shape the agendas of producers (Lundvall 1992a).

Second – and again drawing on the two specific cases – one can see contrasting characteristics that define user–producer interactions. In market interactions, highly intermediated networks serve as a diffusion channel for lead firms, often with producers giving little consideration to the adaptive innovations within such networks, or to how such activity might harm or enhance diffusion of innovations into low-income markets. In contrast, hierarchical interactions can be characterized by elements of technical and managerial regulation which allow large firms some semblance of control over the diffusion of innovations through such sporadic networks.

Greater insights into these contrasting patterns come from drawing on two further concepts – in addition to capabilities – discussed by Lundvall (1992b): power and distance. *Power* balances and control are crucial and were found to be transmitted in a range of more direct and indirect activities, norms, objects, etc. which shape interactions. While power in both types of interaction is heavily skewed towards the lead firm, there may be possibilities for greater freedom for localized innovation in the market mode given the indirect links. *Distance* explains how close users and producers are in geographical, cultural or organizational terms. In this case, the distance is greater in the market than in the hierarchical mode. These twin ideas of power and distance allow some more granular understanding of the connection between users and producers. For example, the absorption of local adaptations – both embodied (i.e. technological adaptations) or disembodied (i.e. best practices and configurations) (Rosenberg 1982) – by producers will be greater where both power inequalities and distance between producer and user are lower.

5.2. *User–producer interaction and outcomes*

Given this outline which helps one to categorize and understand the nature of user–producer interactions, it is possible to discern different learning outcomes from these two interaction modes. When networks are defined as more market-led, learning among demand-side innovation intermediaries tends to focus on adaptation to fit in with local markets. Being indirectly connected to producers, the inherent inequality between intermediaries and lead firms means that local adaptations are limited in their reverse flows back to distant larger firms. Thus, as outlined in the handset case, local adaptations tend to spread through idiosyncratic adaptation, spillover effects and imitation, rather than directly through the networks (Pietrobelli and Rabellotti 2011).

In contrast, where user–producer interactions are more hierarchical, learning comes in 'deliberate' knowledge transfer activities through networks. However, given the importance of demand-based learning and localized innovation in such unique (and often less-well understood) low-income markets, there is a risk of top-down control, with producer dominance restricting learning to a one-way top-down flow. This reduces the ability of local actors to learn and innovate in response to their particular local context, due to the constraints that are placed upon them.

Thus, each mode has its own risks that limit inclusive innovation. A marketized approach risks unchecked localized innovation on the demand side, which does not flow back to producers. With a lack of oversight, this might lead to inconsistent quality and sometimes undesirable forms of innovation locally, which producers have less power to stop. For producers, insufficient user–producer interactions risk reducing understanding of low-income markets and hampering their ability to innovate specifically for those markets. For hierarchical interactions, an excess of guidance leads to a risk of mismatch between localized needs of innovation and top-down forms, where demand-side interactions are limited in the range of localized innovation available, and hence there is lower scope for local actors to be able to adapt appropriately for their local markets.

5.3. *Suggested approaches*

The contrasting modes of interaction seen in these cases may derive from their institutional characteristics: the particular technologies, external regulations, or actors involved.[5] M-Pesa is a centrally controlled ICT service: the nature of financial transactions and consequent strict regulatory requirements inevitably support growing elements of technical control in such a network. Further, the important role of agents combined with the complexity of agent requirements implies strong oversight as a natural outcome of service conditions. Increased monitoring and control are inevitable in some senses from such a combination of factors. Similarly in the handset sub-sector, mobile phones are seen by lead firms as technical objects, not services, which can simply be retailed downstream. Thus, the nature of the innovation creates fewer needs for checks, balances and regulations when compared to M-Pesa. Further, in Kenya the historical presence of importing as a specialism of the Somali and Indian communities has driven growth of increasingly reconfigurable and intermediated relations via informal channels in the handset sub-sector.

These institutional characteristics mean – to some extent – the nature of relations, interactions and risks are predetermined in relation to any given inclusive innovation. However, as emphasized in both cases, a predetermination of risk does not mean an inevitability of outcome. Actions both bottom-up and top-down to refine the nature of relations have had considerable effect on learning and innovation in the system. The key three explanators introduced previously – *capabilities on the demand side*, *power* and *distance* – can provide insight here.

Building *capabilities on the demand side* is likely to revolve around the presence and position of local intermediaries, and the knowledge that emerges from these actors which can be a crucial resource to support effective inclusive innovation. Thus, nurturing these actors can amplify voice and localized adaptations of/for their users. For instance, in the handset sub-sector, the popularity of several smaller handset firms can be linked to their adaptation and support for wholesalers and sellers, with a much more active staff interacting to nurture these sellers.

Hierarchical interactions with an excess of top-down *power* may benefit from purposive activity which reduces the volume of indirect elements of managerial and technical control. This provides more leeway for localized innovation to occur, allowing more room for local independence and learning. For instance, with M-Pesa, when dealers were given some leeway to adapt their business models for low-income markets, this resulted in new service delivery innovation around the so-called 'sub-agent model' which became a core driver of inclusive innovation in terms of the M-Pesa service (Foster and Heeks 2013b).

In less coherent market networks, attempts at disintermediation can allow producers to move closer towards users and improve circular flows of knowledge and learning. Stronger relations are likely to be enhanced where *distance* between producers and low-income markets is smaller. In terms of geographical distance, closer connection can allow more interactive links. So too with cultural distance, where cultural similarities and connection can serve to build clear mutual understanding between users and producers. Finally, organizational distance can be reduced if producer firms vertically integrate elements of networks, thus absorbing some of the sites of learning and innovation within the network. This was the case in mobile handset firms, when more active focus, marketing and phone model adaptation in Kenya aligned with the shift of operations staff away from overseas to local offices, providing a more nuanced understanding of what was going on among low-income actors.

6. Conclusion

There is a growing body of literature on inclusive innovation but it has tended to divide into two camps. Base-of-the-pyramid literature has emphasized top-down innovation by lead firms, with local micro-enterprise seen only through that lens. Emerging literature on bottom-up adaptive innovation by localized actors based in and around low-income communities has given little thought to wider factors. For inclusive innovation, as demonstrated by the cases outlined here, it is not a case of 'either/or'. Activities which successfully cohere top-down and bottom-up activities – in successful interchange of knowledge and learning – will help scale innovations; disconnection will do the opposite. Thus, this work highlights a key direction of future research which emphasizes and expands on the *interactive* nature of knowledge and learning for inclusive innovation.

Lundvall's model of user–producer interaction provides a starting point for understanding those connections but, in line with the predictions of Figure 2, it needs modification to encompass the particular nature of innovation for low-income consumers (e.g. its diversity, atomization, informality) and the longer chains of intermediation that sit between user and producer. The case analysis undertaken here offers further insights into the modification of user–producer interaction and its implication for inclusive innovation systems, as summarized in Figure 5.

As shown at the top of the figure, we can characterize user–producer interaction in such situations in terms of three explanators: demand-side capability, power/control and distance. These characteristics differ somewhat between two modes of interaction found in practice – hierarchical and market-based. Almost all inclusive innovation systems contain some element of hierarchy and some element of market-based transaction. However, the emphasis in the two case studies was sufficient to differentiate them along this continuum, with consequent differences in learning and ultimately in innovation, as shown in the mid-section of Figure 5.

While to some extent predetermined, the outcomes of these user–producer interactions are not set in stone, and the case analysis derived some pointers on improving those interactions. These particularly related to the inherent risks that come from both modes, and to interventions that can shape the core variables, as summarized at the bottom of Figure 5.

For large firms interested in low-income markets, intentionally nurturing user–producer interactions within supply networks – by supporting and operationally connecting to demand-side intermediaries, and by balancing elements of power in relations – can be beneficial. Reducing distance can enhance knowledge that lead firms can ingest about the needs of low-income users.

For those interested in the value of locally innovative activities within communities, we have seen that the nature of interactions around diffused innovations often determines how such innovations are able (or not) to be adapted. This in turn determines the extent to which innovations are diffused and adopted. Interventions that enhance the voice of low-income

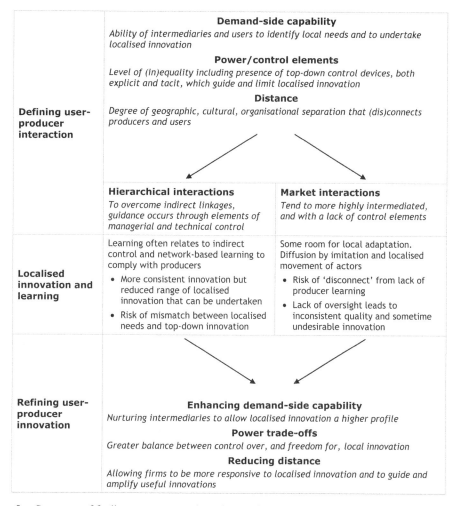

Figure 5.   Summary of findings on user–producer interaction in the two cases.

innovators, and those which dissipate top-down control might be used as ways of expanding the range of localized innovation, thus increasing the long-term inclusivity of both innovation process and products.

Notes

1. Agents in M-Pesa allow customers to convert between virtual e-cash of the mobile transfer service and real money. There were 27,988 M-Pesa agents in Kenya as of April 2011 (Safaricom 2011).
2. This was one of the security measures introduced into the service as part of 'anti-money laundering' and 'know your customer' rules, which came to form a core element of agent service.
3. This includes those who cannot afford the fee for identification, those who do not have documentation such as birth certificates, and those who are illegal immigrants.
4. Transactions in the M-Pesa service are charged on a sliding scale of commission depending on the amount transacted.
5. A derivation in part supported in wider literature examining the underlying nature of innovation networks and in systems of innovation notions of 'path-dependency' (Nelson and Rosenberg 1993).

References

Altenburg, T. 2009. "Building Inclusive Innovation Systems in Developing Countries: Challenges for IS Research." In *Handbook on Innovation Systems and Developing Countries: Building Domestic Capabilities in a Global Context*, edited by B. A. Lundvall, K. J. Joseph, and C. Chaminade, 33–56. Cheltenham: Edward Elgar.

Anderson, J., and M. Kupp. 2008. "Serving the Poor: Drivers of Business Model Innovation in Mobile." *Info* 10 (1): 5–12.

Arocena, R., and J. Sutz. 2000. "Looking at National Systems of Innovation from the South." *Industry & Innovation* 7 (1): 55–75.

Arora, S., and H. Romijn. 2013. "The Empty Rhetoric of Poverty Reduction at the Base of the Pyramid." *Organization* 19 (4): 481–505.

Berdegué, J. A. 2005. *Pro-Poor Innovation Systems*. Background Paper. Rome: IFAD.

Chataway, J., K. Chaturvedi, R. Hanlin, J. Mugwagwa, J. Smith, and D. Wield. 2009. "Building the Case for Systems of Health Innovation in Africa." In *Science, Technology and Innovation for Public Health in Africa*, edited by F. Kalua, A. Awotedu, L. Kamwanja, and J. Saka, 7–52. Pretoria: NEPAD.

Clark, N. 2002. "Innovation Systems, Institutional Change and the New Knowledge Market: Implications for Third World Agricultural Development." *Economics of Innovation and New Technology* 11 (4–5): 353–368.

Cozzens, S. E., and R. Kaplinsky. 2009. "Innovation, Poverty and Inequality: Cause, Coincidence or Co-Evolution?." In *Handbook on Innovation Systems and Developing Countries: Building Domestic Capabilities in a Global Context*, edited by B. A. Lundvall, K. J. Joseph, and C. Chaminade, 57–83. Cheltenham: Edward Elgar.

Cozzens, S. E., and J. Sutz. 2012. *Innovation in Informal Settings: A Research Agenda*. Ottawa: International Development Research Centre.

Edquist, C. 1997. *Systems of Innovation Technologies, Institutions and Organisations*. London: Pinter.

Foster, C., and R. Heeks. 2013a. "Conceptualising Inclusive Innovation: Modifying Systems of Innovation Frameworks to Understand Diffusion of New Technology to Low-Income Consumers." *European Journal of Development Research* 25 (3): 333–355.

Foster, C., and R. Heeks. 2013b. "Innovation and Scaling of ICT for the Bottom-of-the-Pyramid." *Journal of Information Technology* 28 (4): 296–315.

Freeman, C. 1995. "The National System of Innovation in Historical Perspective." *Cambridge Journal of Economics* 19 (1): 5–24.

Hart, S. L., and C. M. Christensen. 2002. "The Great Leap: Driving Innovation from the Base of the Pyramid." *MIT Sloan Management Review* 44 (1): 51–56.

Hart, S. L., and T. London. 2005. "Developing Native Capability: What Multinational Corporations Can Learn from the Base of the Pyramid." *Stanford Social Innovation Review* 3 (2): 28–33.

Heeks, R., M. Amalia, R. Kintu, and N. Shah. 2013. *Inclusive Innovation: Definition, Conceptualisation and Future Research Priorities*. Development Informatics Working Paper 53. Manchester: University of Manchester.

Howells, J. 2006. "Intermediation and the Role of Intermediaries in Innovation." *Research Policy* 35 (5): 715–728.

Hughes, N., and S. Lonie. 2007. "M-PESA: Mobile Money for the 'Unbanked' Turning Cellphones into 24-Hour Tellers in Kenya." *Innovations* 2 (1–2): 63–81.

Jack, W., and T. Suri. 2010. *The Economics of M-Pesa: An Update*. Boston, MA: MIT Sloan.

Kaplinsky, R., J. Chataway, R. Hanlin, D. Kale, L. Muraguri, T. Papaioannou, P. Robbins, and W. Wamae. 2009. "Below the Radar: What Does Innovation in Emerging Economies Have to Offer Other Low-Income Economies?." *International Journal of Technology Management and Sustainable Development* 8 (3): 177–197.

Kraemer-Mbula, E., and W. Wamae. 2010. *Innovation and the Development Agenda*. Paris: OECD/IDRC.

London, T., R. Anupindi, and S. Sheth. 2010. "Creating Mutual Value: Lessons Learned from Ventures Serving Base of the Pyramid Producers." *Journal of Business Research* 63 (6): 582–594.

London, T., and S. L. Hart. 2004. "Reinventing Strategies for Emerging Markets: Beyond the Transnational Model." *Journal of International Business Studies* 35 (5): 350–370.

Lundvall, B. A. 1988. "Innovation as an Interactive Process: From User–Producer Interaction to the National System of Innovation." In *Technical Change and Economic Theory*, edited by G. Dosi, C. Freeman, R. R. Nelson, G. Silverberg, and L. L. Soete, 349–370. London: Pinter.

Lundvall, B. A. 1992a. "User–Producer Relationships, National Systems of Innovation and Internationalisation." In *National Systems of Innovation: Towards a Theory of Innovation and Interactive Learning*, edited by B. A. Lundvall, 45–67. London: Pinter.

Lundvall, B. A., ed. 1992b. *National Systems of Innovation: Toward a Theory of Innovation and Interactive Learning*. London: Pinter.

Lundvall, B. A. 2011. "Notes on Innovation Systems and Economic Development." *Innovation and Development* 1 (1): 25–38.

Lundvall, B. A., and P. Intarakumnerd. 2006. *Asia's Innovation Systems in Transition*. Cheltenham: Edward Elgar.

Lundvall, B. A., K. J. Joseph, and C. Chaminade. 2009. *Handbook on Innovation Systems and Developing Countries: Building Domestic Capabilities in a Global Context*. Cheltenham: Edward Elgar.

Lundvall, B. A., J. Vang, K. J. Joseph, and C. Chaminade. 2009. "Innovation System Research and Developing Countries." In *Handbook on Innovation Systems and Developing Countries: Building Domestic Capabilities in a Global Context*, edited by B. A. Lundvall, K. J. Joseph, and C. Chaminade, 1–32. Cheltenham: Edward Elgar.

Mugabe, J. O. 2005. *Health Innovation Systems in Developing Countries. Strategies for Building Scientific and Technological Capacities*. Background Paper prepared for the Commission on Intellectual Property, Innovation and Public Health. Geneva, Switzerland: World Health Organisation.

Nahuis, R., E. H. M. Moors, and R. Smits. 2009. *User Producer Interaction in Context: A Classification*, ISU Working Paper, 09.01. Utrecht, Netherlands: Utrecht University.

Nelson, R. R., and N. Rosenberg. 1993. *Technical Innovation and National Systems*. New York: Oxford University Press.

Neuman, W. L. 2011. *Social Research Methods: Qualitative and Quantitative Approaches*. Boston, MA: Allyn & Bacon.

Pietrobelli, C., and R. Rabellotti. 2011. "Global Value Chains Meet Innovation Systems: Are There Learning Opportunities for Developing Countries?" *World Development* 39 (7): 1261–1269.

Prahalad, C. K. 2006. "The Innovation Sandbox." *Strategy and Business* 44: 62–71.

Prahalad, C. K. 2009. *The Fortune at the Bottom of the Pyramid: Eradicating Poverty Through Profits*. 5th Anniversary ed. Philadelphia: Wharton School Publishing.

Rosenberg, N. 1982. *Inside the Black Box: Technology and Economics*. Cambridge, UK: Cambridge University Press.

Safaricom. 2011. *M-PESA Customer and Agent Numbers*. Nairobi, Kenya: Safaricom. Accessed March 20, 2012. http://www.safaricom.co.ke/index.php?id=1073

Simanis, E., and S. Hart. 2009. "Innovation from the Inside Out." *MIT Sloan Management Review* 50 (4): 78–86.

Singh, R., V. Gupta, and A. Mondal. 2011. *JUGAAD – Not Just "Making Do" but a Low Cost Survival & Coping Strategy at the Bottom of the Pyramids*, Working Paper Series no. 677. Kolkata, India: Indian Institute of Management Calcutta.

Spielman, D. J., J. Ekboir, and K. Davis. 2009. "The Art and Science of Innovation Systems Inquiry: Applications to Sub-Saharan African Agriculture." *Technology in Society* 31 (4): 399–405.

Stewart, J., and S. Hyysalo. 2008. "Intermediaries, Users and Social Learning in Technological Innovation." *International Journal of Innovation Management* 12 (3): 295–325.

Stuart, G., and M. Cohen. 2011. *Cash In, Cash Out Kenya: The Role of M-PESA in the Lives of Low Income People*. College Park, MD: IRIS Center, University of Maryland.

Sumberg, J. 2005. "Systems of Innovation Theory and the Changing Architecture of Agricultural Research in Africa." *Food Policy* 30 (1): 21–41.

Utz, A., and C. Dahlman. 2007. "Promoting Inclusive Innovation." In *Unleashing India's Innovation: Toward Sustainable and Inclusive Growth*, edited by M. A. Dutz, 105–128. Washington, DC: World Bank.

World Bank. 2011. *Global Financial Inclusion (Global Findex) Database*. Washington, DC: World Bank.

Operationalizing inclusive innovation: lessons from innovation platforms in livestock value chains in India and Mozambique

Kees Swaans[a], Birgit Boogaard[b], Ramkumar Bendapudi[c], Hailemichael Taye[a], Saskia Hendrickx[b] and Laurens Klerkx[d]

[a]International Livestock Research Institute (ILRI), Addis Ababa, Ethiopia; [b]ILRI, Maputo, Mozambique; [c]ILRI, Delhi, India; [d]Knowledge, Technology and Innovation Group, Wageningen University, Wageningen, The Netherlands

Various authors have identified the potential relevance of innovation system approaches for inclusive innovation, that is, the means by which new goods and services are developed for and by the poor. However, it is still a question how best to operationalize this. Innovation platforms (IPs) represent an example of putting an inclusive innovation system approach into practice by bringing different types of stakeholders together to address issues of mutual concern and interest with a specific focus on the marginalized poor. This paper explores the formation and functioning of IPs with the aim of providing lessons on the conditions and factors that play a role in making them effective. The study shows the importance of social organization, representation, and incentives to ensure a 'true' participatory innovation process, which is based on demand and embedded in the context. Critical to this is a flexible planning process stimulating incremental change through so-called innovation bundles (i.e. combinations of technological, organizational, and institutional innovations) and reflexive learning (systematically challenging constraining factors). Furthermore, local institutions embedded in norms and values are crucial to understand people's decisions. Due to weak linkages between value chain actors, innovation brokers have a vital role in facilitating the innovation process. Overall, IPs are a promising model for inclusive innovation, but they require a careful assessment of and adjustment to the institutional context.

1. Introduction

Innovation and technological change can play an important role in poverty reduction, but conventional approaches have failed to deliver for the poor (Leeuwis and van den Ban 2004; Cozzens and Sutz 2014). This is most striking in the agricultural sector, the main source of livelihood for the majority of the worlds' poorest population. The structures and processes required to develop and deliver new goods and services incorporating the needs and interests of the poor are increasingly known as 'inclusive innovation' (Foster and Heeks 2013a). Inclusive innovation approaches are a response to generic innovation system approaches which do not sufficiently consider that inclusivity of the poor in the process of innovation (e.g. the involvement of poor community members in design and development) and inclusivity of output of innovation processes (e.g. the development, production, and delivery of goods and services that are appropriate to the needs of the poor) are essential for development (Foster and Heeks 2013b; Cozzens and Sutz 2014). Also in agriculture, this is the case: there is an increasing interest in using a 'value chain approach' to reach development objectives, but market failures often result in suboptimal performance of the chain and limited participation of the poor (Vorley, del Pozo-Vergnes, and Barnett 2012).[1] Furthermore, in agriculture, there has been for a long time a focus on transfer of technologies aimed at solving particular technological problems at the farm level (e.g. pest management), without considering that inclusive innovation requires several significant changes in the broader setting in which smallholder farms are embedded, such as land tenure arrangements, input markets, and service provision markets (Hounkonnou et al. 2012).

In recent years, innovation platforms (IPs) – spaces which allow individuals and organizations to come together to address issues of mutual concern and interest – have been promoted as a mechanism to stimulate inclusive innovation in the context of agricultural value chains (van Rooyen and Homann-Kee Tui 2009; Nederlof, Wongtschowski, and van der Lee 2011; Ayele et al. 2012). IPs are based on innovation systems thinking: a holistic and comprehensive framework for understanding innovation as emerging from a broad network of dynamically linked actors within a particular institutional context (see Lundvall 2011, for an analysis of the development of this concept and its relevance for developing countries, and Klerkx, Mierlo, and Leeuwis 2012, for an overview of evolution of this thinking in agriculture). Although various authors have identified the potential relevance of innovation system approaches for inclusive innovation, there is still a question of how best to operationalize this and how to create appropriate policies and interventions to stimulate inclusive innovation (see Foster and Heeks 2013a, 2013b). By investigating the formation and functioning of IPs in a project on pro-poor small ruminant value chains in semi-arid areas in India and Mozambique, we hope to provide some key lessons on the conditions and factors that play a role in making them effective.

This paper is organized as follows. First, a description of the conceptual framework is given in Section 2, before introducing the case study in Section 3. In Sections 4 and 5, we will present the methodology and main findings. Finally, the findings will be discussed in relation to key concepts of inclusive innovation and recommendations are derived.

2. Conceptual framework

2.1. *IPs and inclusive innovation*

Innovation in its broadest sense covers the activities and processes associated with the generation, distribution, and use of new knowledge, which can be technological, organizational, and institutional (Leeuwis and van den Ban 2004). In agriculture, technological innovation refers to all sorts of biotic and abiotic artefacts and practices (e.g. new seeds, animal breeds, machinery, cultivation techniques), whereas organizational and institutional elements involve novel social arrangements (e.g. new forms of labour organization, marketing arrangements, community action; and new or revised institutional set-ups, legal arrangements, and policies) (Leeuwis and van den Ban 2004; Nederlof, Wongtschowski, and van der Lee 2011).

Innovation can be stimulated by learning emerging from relevant networks of actors working together based on some mutually agreed institutional arrangements. In generic innovation literature, concepts such as strategic alliances and innovation networks have been used to indicate this process (Pittaway et al. 2004). In the agricultural sector, such multi-actor arrangements have been captured as IPs (Nederlof, Wongtschowski, and van der Lee 2011), as a way to include the poor more explicitly as beneficiaries and as active participants in innovation processes (FARA 2009; Nederlof, Wongtschowski, and van der Lee 2011).

The use of multi-stakeholder platforms emerged in the early 1990s in the agricultural sector, mainly for the purpose of having a space for deliberation, negotiation, and learning to solve complex natural resource management issues (Röling 1994). This concept has been broadened to bringing together stakeholders in various sectors and from different levels of the innovation system, acknowledging, and making use of the diversity in capacity (knowledge, skills, capabilities, and resources). By connecting diverse actors such as farmers, agricultural input suppliers, traders, food processors, researchers, and government officials, who regularly come together to develop a common vision and find ways to achieve their goals, IPs enable and orchestrate co-evolution between technological development and social and institutional changes (Kilelu, Klerkx, and Leeuwis 2013).

There are several key elements of IPs that can be derived from innovation systems literature (see FARA 2009; Njuki et al. 2010; Nederlof, Wongtschowski, and van der Lee 2011; Ngwenya and Hagmann 2011). We can compare these elements against those created for inclusive innovation (Foster and Heeks 2013a) in order to understand the extent to which IPs can be understood as exemplars of inclusive innovation (see Table 1).

As can be seen from Table 1, despite some differences of language and emphasis, there is a strong fit between the tenets of inclusive innovation and the key elements of IPs:

- Scope: although inclusivity is more a process than an output focus for IPs, they look to address development challenges of excluded groups, rather than orient innovation towards profit maximization.
- Innovation: again, IPs focus especially on the innovation process, whereas Foster and Heeks (2013a) look more at the nature of innovations undertaken; but the process is inclusive and participative, and thus driven by an understanding of user needs and context, as inclusive innovation requires.
- Actors: IPs concentrate on the poor as producers, but in a way they are also consumers of certain (technological) innovations; IPs emphasize the dynamics of actor involvement based on need, but generally they are about linking demand and supply, emphasizing the role of intermediaries to facilitate the platforms.
- Learning: although IPs put a stronger emphasis on a systematic and iterative process of learning through reflection, learning basically revolves around interaction, information exchange, and learning by doing as indicated by Foster and Heeks (2013a).
- Relations: while relations in IPs are orchestrated, they also emphasize the role of informal (and formal) relations and flexibility for innovation by the poor.
- Institutions: informal and formal institutions are acknowledged as important structural elements providing constraints to inclusive innovation; IPs see it as an important task to identify these with relevant actors and try to change them over time.

In short, IPs are a way of operationalizing inclusive innovation through facilitating interaction and learning among different actors, which enable reshaping of relations and institutions.

2.2. *Key issues in IP implementation*

For the implementation of an IP, it is useful to make to make a distinction between IP formation and IP functioning (see Njuki et al. 2010). IP formation refers to a phase of design and structuring of the platform, while IP functioning refers to a phase of learning and innovation through regular and iterative planning, action, and reflection, which may lead to shifts in focus and priority. Below

Table 1.   Key elements of IPs related to concepts of inclusive systems of innovation (after Foster and Heeks 2013a).

	Inclusive systems of innovation	IPs
Scope	Development as socio-economic inclusion	Bring relevant actors together to address a (development) issue of common interest, with a specific focus on marginalized groups
Innovation	Incremental innovation with a focus on diffusion processes (local needs oriented, demand- and context-driven, non-technical innovation, reverse innovation)	Stimulate demand- and context-driven innovation (technological, organisational, and institutional) through joint problem solving, making use of diversity among IP members
Actors	Main focus on low-income producers and/or consumers; non-traditional, less formal, demand-side innovators, chain of intermediaries, linking supply and demand	Main focus on poor producers; relevant actors are invited based on scoping and analysis; membership not fixed, but dynamic, based on need; usually intermediaries facilitate and coordinate the platform
Learning	Contextualized (supply, demand, other); learning by interacting and using and doing (learning about diffusion and use; learning about wider social processes including non-instrumental processes; survival and utility-maximization as guides)	Contextualized learning through communication and information exchange among actors and by trying out; learning based on systematic and iterative process of action, monitoring, reflection, and adaptation
Relations	Necessity (but also limitation) of informal, loose, but socialized relations	Linkages established through interactions between members of the platform and other informal/formal actors necessary to achieve the overall objective; interactions are usually facilitated and coordinated
Institutions	Complex institutional terrain of informal and formal; indirect impact of core, formal institutional forces; importance (including potential negative impact) of informal institutions at local level	Key institutional constraints and opportunities are jointly identified and addressed; institutions can be informal and formal

we describe these two phases in more detail, in order to derive key issues for analysing IP formation and functioning.

2.2.1.   *IP formation*

Wennink and Ochola (2011) distinguish three steps in the formation of IPs: scoping, analysis, and planning. Every step has some key aspects that need to be addressed. 'Scoping' refers to the initial effort to narrow down the platform's topic or focus, and to better understand it, along with the context where the platform is to be inserted; this may affect the level of operation (local, national, etc.), the type of stakeholders, and the organization and governance of the platform. 'Analysis' contributes to identification of the knowledge, skills, and interests – including capacity needs, and joint analysis of problems and opportunities related to the topic of the platform. It often includes a stakeholder or network analysis to map the linkages between the different actors in the agricultural innovation system to make sure that all key stakeholders – including the poor and women – are invited (see also FARA 2009). Finally, 'Planning' is related to a further narrowing down of main points raised during the analysis, and agreement on who must do what and when and the development of an action plan (FARA 2009; Nederlof, Wongtschowski, and van der Lee 2011); this also refers to decisions

Table 2. Key parameters for analysing IP formation and functioning.

	Key parameters
IP formation	Inclusion and representation
	Focus, tasks, and roles
	Identification of constraints and opportunities
	Inventory of knowledge, skills, and interests
	Organizational structure and governance
	Resources
IP functioning	Participation, commitment, and ownership
	Information exchange and communication
	Use of diversity in knowledge, skills, and interests
	Systematic planning, action, and reflection
	Capacity building
	Facilitation and management
	Resource mobilization

regarding the modalities of the platform, how exactly and by whom it will be governed, and the use of resources.

2.2.2. *IP functioning*

After rules and modalities for the platform have been set, a routine of regular IP meetings with feedback of agreed-upon actions becomes established (see Njuki et al. 2010; Nederlof, Wongtschowski, and van der Lee 2011); there are a number of issues that are essential for smooth operation of a platform. First, it is important to ensure that members of the platform actively participate, are committed, and feel a sense of ownership of the process. An effective and efficient process of information sharing and communication needs to be in place, taking into account the diversity in knowledge, skills, and interests of actors. To stimulate a culture of continuous learning, an iterative process of planning, action, and reflection has to be established (Nederlof, Wongtschowski, and van der Lee 2011), which is further enhanced through human and institutional capacity building. Facilitation and management have a critical role to play (Ngwenya and Hagmann 2011), often involving a transition from an external-led initiative to a self-organized platform. Resource mobilization, both in terms of human, physical, and financial resources and in terms of endorsement and support, will be crucial to sustain the process beyond the lifetime of the project.

Key parameters for analysing IP formation and functioning are summarized in Table 2.

3. The imGoats project: a case description

The imGoats project was implemented from January 2011 to June 2013 (30 months) with the aim to transform goat production and marketing in semi-arid areas of India and Mozambique to a sound and profitable enterprise and model that would tap into a growing market. The main target beneficiaries of the project were poor goat keepers, both men and women. The overall project was managed by the International Livestock Research Institute (ILRI) and implemented by Bharatiya Agro Industry Foundation (BAIF) and the Cooperative for Assistance and Relief Everywhere (CARE).

The specific project area in India was Rajasthan State with 2600 target households in Jhadol and Sarada blocks of Udaipur district. For logistical reasons, the number of goat keeper groups participating in the IP was limited to those in the radius of 10–12 km from Jhadol town (IP meeting location). This resulted in 18 project villages being part of the platform, covering about 1000 households (88 groups), with 10–15 families per group. In Mozambique, the project targeted 500 households in Inhassoro district of Inhambane Province; this represented about 3800 direct beneficiaries in 18 villages. Goat keepers were organized in 23 producer groups. Key characteristics of the project sites are described in Table 3.

IPs were used to facilitate communication and collaboration and promote joint action and innovation among the actors along the value chain. They followed an iterative process and met – after an intensive formation process – every two to three months to discuss and implement opportunities to improve markets, production and related policy issues (following van Rooyen and Homann-Kee Tui 2009). Figures 1 and 2 provide an overview for, respectively, India and Mozambique of the key issues discussed or decided in IP meetings and the main actions resulting from those in terms of activities undertaken by IP members, research for and on the IP, and capacity building to support initiated activities.

In both countries, producer groups met regularly with the community animal health workers (CAHWs) and there was an increased interaction with other value chain actors (VC actors) through the IPs. Improved linkages between key actors led to various technological, organizational, and institutional innovations (see Table 4).

Table 3. Key characteristics of the IP project sites.

Topic	Udaipur district, India	Inhassoro district, Mozambique
Population density	196/km^2	11/km^2
IP target households	1000	500
Literacy levels	59%	51% (for Mozambique; no information on province or district)
Average annual rainfall	600 mm	600–800 mm
Livelihoods	Small land and livestock holdings (subsistence agriculture); wage labour important source of income	Small land and livestock holdings (subsistence agriculture); crop production main occupation; cattle numbers very low
Main crops	Maize, wheat, barley, chickpea, rape, and mustard	Maize, groundnuts, beans, cassava, and millet
Average goat herd size	6.2 (range 1–16)	8.4 (range 1–30)
Marketing practices	During main festive period (October to December) and ad hoc throughout the year to meet household demands	During festive period (December) and ad hoc throughout the year to meet household demands
Nearest goat market	50 km (Udaipur)	200 km (Massinga)
Main goat value chain constraints	Inferior male breeding goats; limited access to animal health services; low number of goats available for sale; limited knowledge about improved husbandry practices	Low number of goats; limited access to animal health services; lack of organization of producers; lack of infrastructure; limited knowledge about improved husbandry practices
Main value chain actors	Producers; community animal health workers (CAHWs); local traders/ butchers; long distance traders; local pharmacist; Animal Husbandry Department; BAIF; research (ILRI, Veterinary College)	Producers; CAHWs; local traders/ butchers; local retailer; District and Provincial Veterinary Services; CARE; research (ILRI)

Source: internal documents.

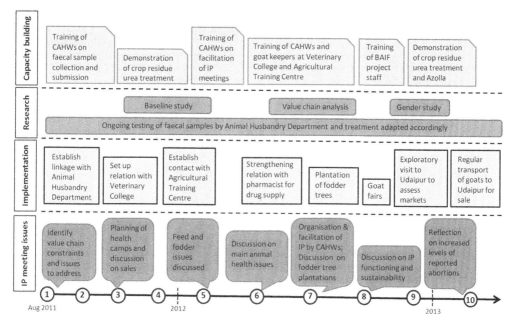

Figure 1. Timeline of IP meetings (O), key issues discussed and resulting activities (implementation, research, and capacity building) in Udaipur district, India.

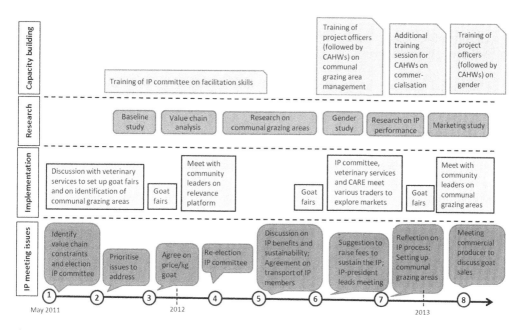

Figure 2. Timeline of IP meetings (O), key issues discussed and resulting activities (implementation, research, and capacity building) in Inhassoro district, Mozambique.

Table 4.   Main innovations in goat value chains as result of IPs in the project areas.

Innovation	Udaipur district, India	Inhassoro district, Mozambique
Technological	Animal health service delivery by CAHWs	Improved goat husbandry practices (watering, feeding, etc.)
	Alternative feeds and new feeding techniques	Improved goat shelters based on local resources
	Better breeding practices (e.g. improved male goats available; castrating inferior male goats)	Animal health service delivery by CAHWs
		Guidelines/training in sustainable communal grazing management based on local situation
Organizational	Aggregation of animals by CAHWs for selling	Aggregation of animals by CAHWs for selling
	Organization of goat fairs and exploring new markets	Organization of goat fairs and exploring new markets
	Organization of health camps for vaccination	Collective management of communal grazing areas
Institutional	IP for actors along the value chain to improve goat production and marketing	IP for actors along the value chain to improve goat production and marketing
	New ways of collaboration between CAHWs and veterinary services for faecal sample testing	Introduction of weighing scales and pre-established live weight price to guarantee a fair price
		Enforcing of existing legislation of communal grazing areas by the district government, including demarcation of areas, and establishment of management associations

The mix of innovations had positive effects on goat management practices, production, and sales. Some key results were:

- In India, goat mortality rates dropped from 30–40% in 2011 to around 10% in March 2013. In Mozambique, the producers also reported a sharp decrease in mortality figures.
- The number of goats increased by at least one or two animals per household in India. There was also anecdotal evidence of increased herd size among producers in Mozambique, but as data collection on production parameters was a challenge, there is no strong evidence for a systematic change across households.
- Data from India further showed that producers were selling more animals: from one animal on average in 2011 to two in 2013, and they received higher prices as a result of increased weight and castrating the males. In Mozambique, producers had also been selling more animals to distant markets, due to a lack of local demand for goats.

4.   Methodology

The research design is a comparative case study based on the imGoats project. A case study allows for an in-depth understanding of the dynamics in the innovation process and multi-stake-holder collaboration (Yin 2003). The study involved participatory observation by two of the authors (RB and BB). Data, mainly qualitative, were collected throughout the project duration (from 2011 to 2013) and the research reported in this paper is based on the analysis of methods used within the context of the IPs themselves. By analysing the innovation process in each case, more insight was gained into the factors and conditions that make IPs effective. The comparison of platforms in two very different settings further enhances the analytical strength of the study.

Various methods were used to analyse IP formation and functioning:

- Review of project documents to understand the context in which the IPs happened.
- IP meeting reports that included: issues discussed and decisions taken, feedback from previous activities and participant lists.
- Recording project progress by mapping behavioural change among VC actors (in terms of relations, practices, and activities).
- Project team reflection exercises to discuss progress made and underlying reasons, held half-way and at the end of the project.

Qualitative data were subjected to thematic content analysis based on the key elements of the analytical framework. To enhance validity of the data, triangulation of various sources and methods was applied. Data analyses and preliminary findings were discussed in-depth amongst the authors. In the course of theorizing, challenging, and making sense of the data observed in the two sites, we have endeavoured to reveal the mechanisms, factors, and conditions that underlie the performance of the IPs.

5. Findings

5.1. *IP formation*

Drawing on the two cases, this section explains the various aspects to consider during IP formation. These aspects (as per Table 2) are: inclusion and representation; a clear focus, tasks, and roles; the identification of constraints and opportunities; an inventory of knowledge, attitudes and skills; organizational structure and governance; and resources.

5.1.1. *Inclusion and representation*

Critical to the IP formation process were the inclusion of the poor and the representation of key actors along the chain. The VC actors in India and Mozambique were identified by respectively BAIF and CARE based on previous experience and consultation. Actors were categorized as producers (goatkeepers and CAHWs), input and service providers (CAHWs, retailer/pharmacist, and veterinary services), post-production actors (mainly traders), and enabling agencies (community leaders, government agencies, CARE/BAIF, and ILRI) (see also Table 3). Membership was flexible, so that new actors could become involved (or existing members leave), based on need.

In India, all participating households in the IP (about 1200; 9% female headed; organized in 88 groups) belonged to Scheduled Tribes, a marginalized group living below the poverty line. Traders were identified based on their interest and through (informal) leadership among traders. In Mozambique, producers (524; 38% women; organized in 23 groups) were selected based on having goats and who had an interest in a goat production and marketing project. However, there were few local traders and private investors in Inhambane Province, making the platform dependent on a small group of actors.

In both countries, there was a clear mechanism for representation of the producer groups in the platform. In India, producer groups were represented by two goat keepers nominated by community members in each village, while CAHWs (serving 100 households, or about

7–10 groups, each) participated as well. In Mozambique, each producer group was asked to elect a representative and a CAHW, which was done in a democratic and participatory way.

5.1.2. *Focus, roles, and tasks*

IPs were found to be the most effective when they had a clear focus with identified roles/tasks for their members. The vision and objective were conceptualized by the project partners at the start of the project and shared at the first IP meeting. However, it was initially difficult for goat producers and other community representatives to think beyond 'production' and to focus on the whole value chain with a commodity focus. During the baseline survey in Mozambique – for logistical reasons initiated after the introduction of the IPs – it became apparent that the main occupation in the area was the cultivation of crops for home consumption with goat husbandry as a low input/ low output side occupation. The commercialization of goats not only required a mental shift among producers and community members, but also a better understanding among the project partners and other actors of the role that goats play in people's livelihoods and farming systems to avoid negative effects.

The lack of common vision building in both countries may also explain that while actors had a clear understanding of their 'position' in the value chain, their roles and tasks (how each actor can contribute to a growing market with win–win situations) were insufficiently explored. For example, the role of traders and government agencies was rather passive/suppor-tive, instead of taking a proactive role, for example, by providing information on markets and consumer preferences and creating incentives for access to inputs and services.

5.1.3. *Identification of constraints and opportunities*

The identification of constraints and opportunities helped to narrow down the focus of the plat-form. In both countries, constraint and opportunity identification was done in a participatory manner facilitated by the project partners. The issues identified were related to production (animal health, husbandry practices, and infrastructure) and marketing (through organization of producers) and were perceived as closely interlinked; in later stages of the project, other con-straints emerged (e.g. lack of feed and water and lack of cash among traders). A drawback was that – partly due to the lack of common vision building and the postponement of the baseline survey (including the value chain analysis) – most of the identified problems and opportunities focused on the producers or production aspects, without further exploring challenges faced along the value chain and among other VC actors, reducing their subsequent interest in the process.

5.1.4. *Identification of knowledge, attitudes, and skills*

As knowledge, attitudes, and skills have implications for planning and innovation processes, it was important to make an inventory of knowledge and skills among actors across the chain at the start of the project. The initial assessment was based on previous experiences of BAIF/CARE; this was later supplemented with information from the baseline study, providing more insights into the context and specific needs of producers. In both countries, producers had limited knowledge and skills of goat husbandry practices and had had minimal training on production and marketing, which made it challenging to move from irregular ad hoc emergency sales to a pattern of regular sales. Moreover, no formal ex ante assessment was held or planned on knowledge, skills, and capacities among other VC actors. This made it difficult to identify opportunities for addressing constraints from within the system and which could have enhanced a feeling of mutual dependency and ownership.

5.1.5. *Organizational structure and governance*

In both countries, IPs were newly established. BAIF/CARE and ILRI took the lead in the initial stages in facilitating and coordinating the IP meetings, but mechanisms were put in place to hand this over to local actors to sustain the innovation process after the project would end. In India, it was envisaged that CAHWs would take over this role; in Mozambique, a committee of four IP members was elected. The frequency of IP meetings was set by the IP members at an interval of every two months. In India, the meeting was at a fixed location, while in Mozambique the location varied. However, as regards ownership, it was a challenge to develop this among local actors who did not have experience with IPs, while documented experience on how to facilitate self-organization in IPs was limited.

5.1.6. *Resources*

Resources for the platform were provided by project funding through BAIF and CARE, which included mainly human resources, but also expenses incurred on transportation and refreshments. In Mozambique, participants were collected by car as locations were spread out. It was the intention to stop providing transport after the first meeting, but in practice, this decision was only taken in the fifth meeting after a discussion on sustainability of the platform among the IP members.

The key findings of the IP formation process are summarized in Box 1.

Box 1. Summary of the IP formation process

- The IP formation process was inclusive: all VC actors were represented; mechanisms were put in place for representation of producer groups.
- The vision and objective were conceptualized by the project partners; potential tasks/ roles of some VC actors in the innovation process were insufficiently explored.
- Problem identification was participatory with a focus on production and marketing; key constraints were closely interlinked.
- Assessment of knowledge/skills among producers and CAHWs was thoroughly explored, but no assessment was planned among other VC actors.
- Project partners took the lead in facilitation and management of the IPs; mechanisms were established to hand this over to local actors.
- Resources were provided through project funding.

5.2. *IP functioning*

After the rules and modalities of the platform have been set, a routine of regular IP meetings with feedback on agreed actions becomes established. Key processes that determine IP functioning are (as per Table 2): participation, commitment, and ownership; information sharing and communication; use of the diversity of knowledge and skills; a systematic process of planning, action, and reflection; capacity building; facilitation and management; and resource mobilization. In this section, we assess how these processes were designed and applied in the case studies.

5.2.1. *Participation, commitment, and ownership*

For a well-functioning IP, the members need to participate actively, be committed to a common cause, and perceive the process as their own. Project reports showed that there was a continuous effort to keep different VC actors involved. In both countries, producers were well represented in the meetings, but there was also large inconsistency in terms of who participated. In India, other activities and events (onset of cropping season, religious festivals) interfered, while in Mozambique, the change in meeting locations played a role. Moreover, in Mozambique, the average number of producers dropped after the fifth meeting, most likely due to a combination of the decision to stop providing transport and unclear incentives for participants; when in the eighth IP meeting, a private investor was involved with potential to buy goats, the number of producers – coming to the meeting by their own transport – increased again. CAHWs and government officials had been active throughout the process; BAIF and CARE worked closely with the CAHWs as service provider and link between the platforms and producer groups, and maintained regular contact with the government agencies.

The involvement of traders and women was, however, problematic. In India, the traders who participated in the first IP meeting made it clear that they would be available in case there are goats to be sold but they did not see the need for their participation in every meeting. Also in Mozambique, traders were initially interested and stimulated the organization of producers, which allowed them to buy an agreed amount of goats at certain dates. However, after the first few goat fairs, their interest faded as demand for goats was lower than anticipated. Also participation of women in the IP meetings was low. Women were mainly found in the producer groups and not among other VC actors. In India, low participation was generally due to the local cultural setting whereby traditionally women are not allowed to leave their community. In Mozambique, initially women participated, but the number decreased after a few IP meetings. This may have been related to an increased interest of community leaders to participate, possibly replacing the female participants as representative for the community. The strong focus on commercialization and marketing – which are considered men's tasks – and the burden of domestic chores may also have played a role.

5.2.2. *Communication and information exchange*

To enhance innovation, effective and efficient communication and knowledge sharing are important, not only between IP members but also beyond the platform. In both countries, information on goat management practices and marketing, constraints, and opportunities was well communicated and shared among VC actors within the platform. CAHWs also shared information with producers during regular group meetings, but there was limited input from the groups regarding issues to be discussed at the platform. As a result of the interventions, information flows between producers and government were strengthened, although the information flow with traders remained rather difficult (slightly better in India compared to Mozambique).

5.2.3. *Use of diversity in knowledge and skills*

There were several specific actions throughout the innovation process that can be related to the use of knowledge/skills of different VC actors (although these were not assessed explicitly ex ante). In India, IP meetings were used to tap into the knowledge from the veterinarian to act on issues that emerged during the meeting; it also exposed CAHWs to a systematic approach to faecal sample testing to identify worm-loads before taking up de-worming. Apart from this, information from the pharmacist was also used to understand what medicines were locally available and what could be ordered in bulk in case the CAHWs wanted to make the purchases collectively. Also in terms of marketing, awareness among the producers and CAHWs increased because of interactions with traders (even if limited) and while preparing action plans to conduct goat fairs or organizing exposure-cum-sale visits to markets in the nearest town. In the case of Mozambique, producers' knowledge and practices on grazing areas were assessed for the development of communal pasture, while subsequently local government, community leaders, and CAHWs provided knowledge for the identification and legislation of communal pasture areas. In addition, five model farmers were identified to share their experiences to other producers, for example, with improved shelters and the provision of water to goats on a regular basis. In general, though, there was less attention to the diversity in knowledge and skills within each group of VC actors and how these could have been exploited.

5.2.4. *Systematic planning, action, and reflection*

In both countries, IP meetings were characterized by a systematic and iterative process of planning, action, reflection, and adaptation. But while some innovation processes were highly predictable, others were unforeseen and unexpected (see Boogaard et al. 2013, for Mozambique). For example, in both countries, access to animal health services was addressed through technological and organizational innovations. These interventions were relatively straightforward and required limited changes in existing extension and training models.

Improving market access was more complicated and included a combination of organizational (aggregation of animals, organization of goat fairs) and institutional elements (the introduction of weighing scales and a pre-established live weight price to guarantee a fair price). In both countries, the organization of goat markets was tried with mixed results and alternative sales strategies were explored (in India, producers started transporting animals to Udaipur and in Mozambique, a private investor and a slaughterhouse were approached). Even less predictable and unforeseen was the development of communal grazing areas in Mozambique. Most goats in Inhassoro District were tethered even though grazing areas were present in the district. The IP members identified the need for communal grazing areas in an IP meeting. The innovation required an integrated package of technological (new management techniques), organizational (collective action between smallholders, community leaders, CAHWs, and local government), and institutional interventions (legalisation of the areas by the district government, including demarcation of the area, and the establishment of associations in the communities which were legally responsible for the areas). Planning in this case was more flexible and adapted in response to daily activities of project staff and IP members.

In the case of Mozambique, there were also regular reflections with members of the platform on the IP process itself; although increased insight did not lead to drastic changes in terms of goals and strategy, some changes were made in terms of the design (e.g. it was decided to stop providing transport and choose a central location for the meeting after the fifth meeting).

5.2.5. *Capacity building*

Capacity building was one of the core elements to further improve the innovation process. Capacity building was based on existing experiences from BAIF and CARE, which were further informed by the baseline surveys and issues that emerged during the IP process. Gaps in knowledge were addressed through specific training sessions and exchange and exposure visits with support from government training institutes and project partners. In both countries, the focus was mainly on producers and CAHWs. In India, sessions were provided on animal health and alternative feeds and feeding techniques, whereas in Mozambique, training concentrated on the management of goats, communal grazing area management, and commercialization of goats. Exchange visits took place between producer groups, while some of the IP members visited potential new traders and markets. Besides the conventional training and exchange/exposure visits, also the exchange of information between members of the platform itself was seen as an important source for learning. This was often informed by feedback of research results, for example, on baseline surveys and studies on specific topics (e.g. on communal grazing areas); crucial in this respect was the timely feedback and the development of easy understandable flyers with key findings and graphics.

CAHWs (India) and IP committee members (Mozambique) were further trained in the facilitation of IPs, while staff from BAIF/CARE received additional sessions on goat management practices and/or gender. What was lacking though was the identification of training needs among other actors. This may have negatively affected the innovation process. For example, in the case of Mozambique, it was assumed that traders had interest in buying goats and a certain degree of entrepreneurial skills. A marketing study in Mozambique revealed, however, that local traders were largely unaware of consumer preferences and behaviour.

5.2.6. *Facilitation and management*

The management process within the IP can be seen as the role of innovation brokers, defined as the persons and organizations that catalyse innovation by bringing actors together and facilitating their interaction (Klerkx, Hall, and Leeuwis 2009). BAIF/CARE and ILRI were responsible for the implementation and facilitation of the IP. However, in addition to the main purpose of innovation brokers – to create linkages and facilitate multi-actor interaction in innovation – they also conducted activities related to strategic networking, technical backstopping, mediation, advocacy, capacity building, and reporting. ILRI postdoctoral researchers played a significant role in terms of research and documentation. The research element was new to BAIF and CARE and played an important role in improved understanding of the local context and in identification of constraints and solutions.

The multiple roles of BAIF/CARE and ILRI within the project revealed their active dynamism that allowed them to adapt to new challenges. IP facilitation and management were gradually handed over to IP members, but this needed a lot of guidance. For these reasons, most of the decisions related to the design of the platform were influenced by former experiences of BAIF/CARE and ILRI.

5.2.7. *Resource mobilization*

Resource mobilization was a strategic concern for the IP functioning and its continuity. IP facilitation and management were highly resource intensive, especially in terms of human resources. It is important to emphasize that the IP was a process, with regular meetings and follow-up; it also included extra efforts to obtain necessary endorsement and support from community leaders and producer groups, while strategic linkages were made with government agencies.

The key findings on IP functioning are summarized in Box 2.

Box 2. Summary of IP functioning

- Participation varied across the VC actors; traders and women were difficult to involve in the innovation process.
- Information flow from platform to producer groups was good, but weak the other way around; CAHWs formed an important link with producers.
- The IP tapped into the knowledge/skills of some VC actors, especially in India; however, diversity in knowledge/skills within each actor group remained largely unexplored.
- Problem solving followed a systematic innovation process, including technological, organizational, and institutional elements; where some interventions were highly predictable, others were not and required flexible planning; in Mozambique, there was a stronger reflection on the IP as an institutional innovation itself.
- Capacity building through training and exposure/exchange visits was important, but the main focus was on producers and CAHWs; IP meetings were also recognized as a form of capacity building through systematic reflection.
- Innovation brokering included multiple diverse tasks; facilitation was gradually handed over to local actors, but project partners continued to play an important role.
- IPs were (human) resource intensive; including extra efforts to get endorsement and support from community leaders and producer groups, and creating strategic linkages with government agencies.

---

6. Discussion

The study showed that IPs can enhance production and marketing by establishing linkages between smallholders and other actors in the value chain. Increased interaction between IP members led to innovations including the introduction and adaptation of goat management practices based on local resources; new forms of organizing producers, production, and marketing; and novel ways of working together with other VC actors. However, the changes in terms of productivity through technical and service delivery interventions and sales were clearer in the case of India, compared to the case from Mozambique. To gain more insight into how innovation system approaches can be made more effective for the poor and enhance inclusive innovation, we analysed the implementation of IPs in terms of IP formation and functioning; here we would like to discuss the main findings of the case study in relation to key concepts of inclusive innovation (i.e. actors, innovation, learning, relations, institutions, and scope; see Table 5).

When we look at the type of actors that were or need to be involved in these instances of inclusive innovation, there are a few key issues worth mentioning. First of all, there is the issue of inclusion and representation. Rules and recruitment of participants may unintentionally lead to exclusion, rather than inclusion (see Swaans et al. 2008). For example, in India, IP meetings were held in Jhadol town, making it difficult for women to attend for cultural reasons. In Mozambique, cost and availability of transport to the meeting venue were a constraining factor. The design and implementation of IPs need to be adapted to and negotiated with the intended beneficiaries. Furthermore, the study showed that especially in Mozambique, the value chain was dependent on a limited set of actors (e.g. in the case of traders), which made

Table 5.   Key issues in IP formation and functioning derived from the case study.

	Key issues in IP formation and functioning
Actors	Rules and regulations (i.e. design) of the platform need to be adapted to include the poor
	Representation of different types of VC actors is critical
	Due to weak linkages between VC actors, intermediaries play a critical role
Innovation	Importance of incentives to ensure demand-driven and contextualized innovation process
	Flexible approach to support incremental change and bundles of innovation (technological, social, and institutional)
	Social organization of producers important for learning and demand articulation
Learning	Learning through interaction and learning by doing; (technical) learning through conventional training, demonstration, and exposure
	Reflexive (transformative) learning by challenging (underlying) critical constraints; important role for research
	Learning/alignment of VC actors to work towards a common cause
Relations	Important to nurture socialized informal (flexible) relations to foster innovation
	Necessary to ensure some consistency in (more formal) relations to reduce risk and uncertainty
	Innovation brokers are critical to link producers to the IP and to establish linkages between VC actors (there may be different intermediaries)
Institutions	Formal institutions (and change thereof) are important to support the innovation process
	Informal institutions such as trust and norms and values are important for people's behaviour, and may require specific methods to address them
Scope	Actors need to feel mutually dependent before engaging them in a process
	Take into account diversity among main beneficiaries when deciding on main focus

it highly vulnerable. The weak linkages between various actors of the value chain made the role of an intermediary for innovation brokering at the initial stages essential.

Innovation in the platforms was strongly demand- and context-driven, but it required a flexible planning process that was able to cater for both predictable and unexpected and unforeseen developments. Like many inclusive innovations, these were not necessarily new, but they were new in the context. Technological innovations were important and made a big difference (e.g. animal treatment, new management practices); but critical to their success was the extent to which these were nurtured and aligned with changes in ways of organization (producer groups, communal grazing areas, health camps, and fairs) and institutions (legislation, rules) (see also Kilelu, Klerkx, and Leeuwis 2013). Organizational innovation was especially important at the producer level; not only to reach economy of scale (through aggregation of animals), but also to stimulate learning and for better demand articulation. A key factor for innovation is the issue of incentives; although this may have been clear for producers, it was less clear for traders/butchers, and shows the importance of the development of business models among the actors in the chain (following Ngwenya and Hagmann 2011).

Learning is critical to any innovation process. Besides the importance of learning through interaction and learning by doing, there were several other types of learning that were important for these inclusive innovations. As knowledge among producers was very limited, conventional learning through training played an important role, including learning through exposure and exchange visits. A form of learning not often mentioned, and which played an important role in the IPs, is reflexive (or transformative) learning (van Mierlo, Arkesteijn, and Leeuwis 2010). Reflexive learning refers to the critical reflection on internal and external factors that constrain people's lives through a systematic process of action and reflection; in the case of the IPs in this study one can think of an improved understanding of the factors that played a role in the marketing of goats, and which helped VC actors to develop new strategies. The study also showed that research, e.g. through value chain analysis and marketing studies, can contribute in revealing these critical factors. Furthermore, learning was important across the chain to ensure that actors were aligned and worked towards a common cause.

In terms of relations, IPs need to be connected to a system that allows for information exchange, experimentation, and learning among producers, for example, through producer groups (see also Ayele et al. 2012). In the two case studies, communication and information exchange among actors within the platforms were well organized, but it proved more difficult to extend this beyond the platform, especially the producer groups. The role of CAHWs as a 'broker' or 'linkage' between the IP and the producer groups was critical. In Mozambique, also model farmers played an important role in mobilizing producers. Although informal socialized relations are important to keep the platform dynamic and able to respond to changes, some form of consistency is desirable to develop reliable relations to reduce uncertainty and risk. Hence, while the study showed the importance of intermediaries to link producers to the platform (e.g. through CAHWs), it also showed the importance of innovation brokers to establish relations with other VC actors (confirming findings by Klerkx, Hall, and Leeuwis 2009; Szogs, Cummings, and Chaminade 2011; Foster and Heeks 2013a).

This brings us to the issues of institutions. Formal institutions were important to support the innovation process, but at least as important were the informal (local) institutions, that is, norms and values on gender and the lack of trust between producers and traders. A group-based approach provides the opportunity to get to know each other, build trust, and stimulate learning; it provides the opportunity to challenge underlying values and relations between stakeholders. However, this may work better in homogeneous settings whereby people feel free to express themselves, than in heterogeneous groups such as an IP; this may particularly be difficult in a value chain context when transactions and competition play an important role. Hence, IPs may need to go along with other forms of interaction at the local level. Also the involvement of champions as role models and support from local leaders was crucial in this respect. To address the way different VC actors work together, requires high-quality facilitation and identification of win–win situations.

Finally, considering the overall focus on socio-economic development, IPs can provide an important mechanism for inclusive innovation but only when actors feel that they are dependent on each other to address certain issues. Moreover, a value chain approach may not be appropriate in every context. In Mozambique, the value chain was very weak or almost non-existent; goats had multiple functions in the households and not everyone – especially women – may have been interested in the commercialization of goats. The IPs did not fully capture this. Under such conditions, alternatives such as a stronger focus on production or diversification of livelihood strategies need to be considered (see Amankwah et al. 2012).

7. Conclusion

From our study, a number of lessons can be drawn as regards using an IP approach to operationalize inclusive innovation. The study shows that social organization, representation, and incentives are important to ensure a 'true' participatory and inclusive innovation process. This requires flexible planning that stimulates incremental change through a mix of technological, organizational, and institutional innovations and (reflexive) learning. Furthermore, a better understanding of local institutions embedded in norms and values is crucial to change people's practices and decisions. Due to the – often – weak linkages among actors in the innovation system, brokers have a vital role to play to facilitate these inclusive innovation processes.

Some key recommendations are: (1) a diagnostic study, including value chain and gender analysis during the inception phase of projects is important to gain a better understanding of the context; (2) the design of IPs and their implementation needs to be adapted to and negotiated with the intended beneficiaries; (3) facilitation by project partners in the initial stages of the IPs may be necessary but handing over to local actors is crucial for continuity and requires time, capacity, and respect from other members of the platform; (4) the complexity of the innovation process requires flexibility from platform members in terms of planning with attention to techno-logical, organizational, and institutional elements; and (5) government decision-makers need to be engaged in the process when appropriate to ensure that innovations are embedded in government strategies and policies.

Overall, IPs are a promising model for operationalizing inclusive innovation, but this requires a careful assessment of and adjustment to the local institutional context. Here also lies a main issue in terms of the scope of inclusive innovation which requires further research, and includes questions such as: Can platforms foster inclusive innovation at a larger scale or are they intrinsi-cally linked to a local context? How do platforms enable broader institutional change for scaling inclusive innovation? What is the cost-effectiveness of IPs vis-à-vis other approaches to inclusive innovation? Answering these questions is key to informing the development of inclusive inno-vation support policies.

Acknowledgements

The authors wish to thank the project teams from BAIF and CARE for sharing their experiences with us. We also wish to thank Alan Duncan (ILRI), Richard Heeks (University of Manchester), Suzan Cozzens (Georgia Institute of Technology), and two anonymous reviewers for their feedback on previous drafts. This article has been written in the context of the 'imGoats' project, financially supported by the Euro-pean Commission through the International Fund for Agricultural Development (IFAD) [grant number C-ECG-45-ILRI].

Note

1. A value chain can be described as the set of actors and activities, and the relationships between them, to develop, produce, deliver, and maintain a product or service; a value chain approach intends to enhance value along the chain by linking supply and demand more effectively (World Bank 2007).

References

Amankwah, K., L. Klerkx, S. J. Oosting, O. Sakyi-Dawson, A. J. van der Zijp, and D. Millar. 2012. "Diagnosing Constraints to Market Participation of Small Ruminant Producers in Northern Ghana: An Innovation Systems Analysis." *NJAS-Wageningen Journal of Life Sciences* 60–63: 37–47. http://dx.doi.org/10.1016/j.njas.2012.06.002

Ayele, S., A. Duncan, A. Larbi, and T. T. Khanh. 2012. "Enhancing Innovation in Livestock Value Chains Through Networks: Lessons from Fodder Innovation Case Studies in Developing Countries." *Science and Public Policy* 39 (3): 333–346.

Boogaard, B. K., K. Swaans, S. C. J. Hendrickx, and M. Cosijn. 2013. "Reflection on Innovation Processes in a Smallholder Goat Development Project in Mozambique." In *Innovation in Smallholder Farming in Africa: Recent Advances and Recommendations*, edited by B. Triomphe, A. Waters-Bayer, L. Klerkx, M. Schut, B. Cullen, G. Kamau, and E. LeBorgne. Proceedings of the workshop on agricultural inno-vation systems in Africa (AISA), Nairobi, Kenya, May 29–31. pp. 67–71.

Cozzens, S., and J. Sutz. 2014. "Innovation in Informal Settings: Reflections and Proposals for a Research Agenda." *Innovation and Development* 4 (1): 5–31.

FARA (Forum for Agricultural Research in Africa). 2009. "Strategy and lessons sharing forum." Synthesis Report. Sub-Saharan Africa Challenge Program (SSA CP). www.fara-africa.org/media/uploads/library/docs/ssacp/Strategy_meeting_final_report16_feb_2010.pdf

Foster, C., and R. Heeks. 2013a. "Conceptualising Inclusive Innovation: Modifying Systems of Innovation Frameworks to Understand Diffusion of New Technology to Low-Income Consumers." *European Journal of Development Research* 25 (3): 333–355.

Foster, C., and R. Heeks. 2013b. "Analyzing Policy for Inclusive Innovation: The Mobile Sector and Base-of-the-pyramid Markets in Kenya." *Innovation and Development* 3 (1): 103–119.

Hounkonnou, D., D. Kossou, T. W. Kuyper, C. Leeuwis, E. S. Nederlof, N. Röling, O. Sakyi-Dawson, M. Traoré, and A. van Huis. 2012. "An Innovation Systems Approach to Institutional Change: Smallholder Development in West Africa." *Agricultural Systems* 108: 74–83. http://dx.doi.org/10.1016/j.agsy.2012.01.007

Kilelu, C. W., L. Klerkx, and C. Leeuwis. 2013. "Unravelling the Role of Innovation Platforms in Supporting Co-evolution of Innovation: Contributions and Tensions in a Smallholder Dairy Development Programme." *Agricultural Systems* 118: 65–77. http://dx.doi.org/10.1016/j.agsy.2013.03.003

Klerkx, L., A. Hall, and C. Leeuwis. 2009. "Strengthening Agricultural Innovation Capacity: Are Innovation Brokers the Answer?" *International Journal of Agricultural Resources, Governance and Ecology* 8 (5/6): 409–438.

Klerkx, L., B. Mierlo, and C. Leeuwis. 2012. "Evolution of Systems Approaches to Agricultural Innovation: Concepts, Analysis and Interventions." In *Farming Systems Research into the 21st Century: The New Dynamic*, edited by I. Darnhofer, D. Gibbon, and B. Dedieu, 457–483. Dordrecht: Springer Netherlands.

Leeuwis, C., and A. van den Ban. 2004. *Communication for Rural Innovation: Rethinking Agricultural Extension*. Oxford: Blackwell Science.

Lundvall, B-Å. 2011. "Notes on Innovation Systems and Economic Development." *Innovation and Development* 1 (1): 25–38.

van Mierlo, B., M. Arkesteijn, and C. Leeuwis. 2010. "Enhancing the Reflexivity of System Innovation Projects with System Analyses." *American Journal of Evaluation* 31 (2): 143–161.

Nederlof, S., M. Wongtschowski, and F. van der Lee. eds. 2011. *Putting Heads Together: Agricultural Innovation Platforms in Practice*. Bulletin 396. Amsterdam: KIT publishers.

Ngwenya, H., and J. Hagmann. 2011. "Making Innovation Systems Work in Practice: Experiences in Integrating Innovation, Social Learning and Knowledge in Innovation Platforms." *Knowledge Management for Development Journal* 7 (1): 109–124.

Njuki, J., P., Pali, K. Nyikihadzoi, P. Olaride, and A. Adekunle. 2010. *Monitoring and Evaluation Strategy for the Sub-Saharan Africa Challenge Program*. Accra: FARA.

Pittaway, L., M. Robertson, K. Munir, D. Denyer, and A. Neely. 2004. "Networking and Innovation: A Systematic Review of the Evidence." *International Journal of Management Reviews* 5 (3–4): 137–168.

Röling, N. 1994. "Platforms for Decision Making About Ecosystems." In *The Future of the Land: Mobilizing and Integrating Knowledge for Land Use Options*, edited by L. O. Fresco, L. Stroosnijder, J. Bouma, and H. van Keulen, 385–393. Chichester: John Wiley and Sons.

van Rooyen, A., and S. Homann-Kee Tui. 2009. "Promoting Goat Market and Technology Development in Semiarid Zimbabwe for Food Security and Income Growth." *Tropical and Subtropical Agroecosystems* 11 (1): 1–5.

Swaans, K., J. E. W. Broerse, M. Salomon, M. Mudhara, M. Mweli, and J. F. G. Bunders. 2008. "The Farmer Life School: Experience from an Innovative Approach to HIV Education Among Farmers in South Africa." *SAHARA J* 5 (2): 52–64.

Szogs, A., A. Cummings, and C. Chaminade. 2011. "Building Systems of Innovation in Less Developed Countries: The Role of Intermediate Organizations Supporting Interactions in Tanzania and El Salvador." *Innovation and Development* 1 (2): 283–302.

Vorley, B., E. del Pozo-Vergnes, and A. Barnett. 2012. *Small Producer Agency in the Globalised Market: Making Choices in a Changing World*. London: IIED; The Hague: HIVOS.

Wennink, B., and W. Ochola. 2011. "Designing Innovation Platforms." In *Putting Heads Together: Agricultural Innovation Platforms in Practice*, edited by S. Nederlof, M. Wongtschowski, and F. van der Lee, 30–42. Bulletin 396. Amsterdam: KIT publishers.

World Bank. 2007. *Enhancing Agricultural Innovation: How to Go beyond the Strengthening of Research Systems*. Washington, DC: World Bank.

Yin, R. K. 2003. *Case Study Research: Design and Methods*. 3rd ed. Thousand Oaks, CA: Sage.

An analysis of power dynamics within innovation platforms for natural resource management

Beth Cullen[a], Josephine Tucker[b], Katherine Snyder[c], Zelalem Lema[a] and Alan Duncan[a]

[a]International Livestock Research Institute, ILRI, Addis Ababa, Ethiopia; [b]Overseas Development Institute, London, UK; [c]International Center for Tropical Agriculture, c/o International Centre of Insect Physiology and Ecology (ICIPE), Nairobi, Kenya

Innovation systems thinking is increasingly influencing approaches to sustainable agricultural development in developing world contexts. This represents a shift away from technology transfer towards recognition that agricultural change entails complex interactions among multiple actors and a range of technical, social and institutional factors. One option for practically applying innovation systems thinking involves the establishment of innovation platforms (IPs). Such platforms are designed to bring together a variety of different stakeholders to exchange knowledge and resources and take action to solve common problems. Yet relatively little is known about how IPs operate in practice, particularly how power dynamics influence platform processes. This paper focuses on a research-for-development project in the Ethiopian highlands which established three IPs for improved natural resource management. The 'power cube' is used to retrospectively analyse the spaces, forms and levels of power within these platforms and the impact on platform processes and resulting interventions. The overall aim is to highlight the importance of power issues in order to better assess the strengths and limitations of IPs as a model for inclusive innovation. Findings suggest that while IPs may achieve some short-term success in creating spaces for wider participation in decision-making processes, they may be significantly influenced by forms of power which may not always be visible or easily challenged.

1. Introduction

In the last 40 years, there has been a shift from linear approaches to technology and knowledge transfer exemplified by the World Bank Training and Visit Program (Anderson, Feder, and Ganguly 2006) to participatory approaches with the Farmer First initiative (Chambers 1994) and recently innovation system approaches. This change is largely due to a growing recognition that agricultural change is not just about adopting new technologies; it entails complex inter-actions among multiple actors and a range of technical, social and institutional factors. In addition, there is greater awareness that the diffusion of agricultural technologies requires loca-lized adaptation and socio-technical innovation to ensure the appropriateness of technologies in specific contexts. This has led to the development of the agricultural innovation systems

(AIS) concept, influenced by ideas from Lundvall (1992) on national systems of innovation and developed by Hall et al. (2001, 2006) within the agricultural research arena (Klerkx, van Mierlo, and Leeuwis 2012, 463).

An innovation system refers to a cluster of individuals and organizations involved in knowledge generation, diffusion and use, together with the processes required to turn knowledge into useful economic or social benefits. Innovation is often defined as 'new information introduced into and utilised in an economic or social process' (Spielman 2005, 12), which may include new combinations of existing knowledge. Innovations may be technological, organizational, institutional, managerial, related to service delivery or to policy. Most importantly, this definition implies that knowledge or technology does not become an innovation unless it is used. Advocates of AIS believe that innovation follows a non-linear process, and that the 'system' capacity depends on the 'density and quality of relationships' between the innovation agents and supporting institutions (Altenburg, Schmitz, and Stamm 2008, 327). Therefore, there is an explicit focus on linkages between actors within the system, and the influence of institutions and infrastructures on these actors' ability to innovate. The focus on actor linkages implies that improved interaction will result in better information exchange, ideas and opportunities and ultimately lead to innovation. However, there have been questions about the best way to achieve these linkages.

AIS thinking prompted experimentation with different methods for establishing and supporting multi-stakeholder innovation. Innovation platforms (IPs) (also referred to as multi-stakeholder platforms, innovation networks or learning alliances) offer one potential approach. IPs are forums that are designed to bring together stakeholders from different interest groups, disciplines, sectors and organizations to exchange knowledge, ideas and resources and take action to solve common problems in order to bring about a desired change. The combination of these different actors is seen as a potential catalyst for addressing problems within a given system, and a way of ensuring that various groups – including those traditionally marginalized from innovation – can contribute to the change process. As such, IPs are often promoted as a means of addressing power imbalances between farming communities and decision-makers, and they can be regarded as a new model of inclusive innovation (see also Swaans et al. 2014).

IPs may also help address the lack of coordination and communication between stakeholders; seen, alongside power imbalances, as a key bottleneck to the process of fostering change in rural systems. Although there is an extensive literature which discusses innovation systems and IPs from a theoretical standpoint to date, there has been limited analysis of how IPs operate in practice (Nederlof, Wongtschowski, and van der Lee 2011, 11). The issue of power dynamics in particular tends to be overlooked. Considering the aims of IPs, and their current popularity, it is important to understand how power dynamics can potentially influence platform processes and in particular the participation of marginalized groups. This may also provide an insight into power relations within inclusive innovation more broadly.

This paper explores the use of IPs for natural resource management (NRM) in the Ethiopian highlands. Three platforms were established as part of a research-for-development project called the Nile Basin Development Challenge (NBDC), funded by the CGIAR[1] Challenge Program on Water and Food (CPWF). The NBDC project aims to improve the resilience of rural livelihoods in the Ethiopian highlands through a landscape approach to NRM. The project approach is based on the premise that development of integrated strategies, by a range of stakeholders, which consider technologies, policies and institutions, will lead to improved NRM. IPs were aimed to provide a forum for negotiation and dialogue to encourage: joint identification of issues; improved linkages between actors; increased community participation in planning processes; and co-design of interventions tailored to local livelihoods, environmental conditions and the needs of different stakeholders.

Power dynamics between platform members, competing interests, difficulties identifying and aligning incentives for collective action, as well as the wider political and institutional context, presented particular challenges for platform facilitation and had significant repercussions for the IP interventions. Below, these are described in order to highlight why a more in-depth understanding of power dynamics is important for future IP processes. This will provide valuable insights for NRM and for inclusive innovation, in both of which power remains an often neglected topic. Yet in both cases, power shapes institutional arrangements which create differentiated access to and control over resources. This, in turn, can create differentiated outcomes of innovation and development processes.

The paper is organized in the following way: Section 2 reviews work to date on power dynamics within multi-stakeholder platforms and briefly introduces the power cube conceptual framework. Sections 3 and 4 describe the research methods and the Ethiopian context. Section 5, containing the results and discussion, uses the power cube as an organizing framework and is divided into subsections on 'IPs as spaces for participation', 'forms of power within the platform space' and 'levels of power'. The concluding Section 6 summarizes the findings and their implications.

2. Conceptual framework

The politics of participation and the role of power dynamics within participatory processes have been extensively written about. Indeed, the twenty-first century has witnessed a growing backlash against 'participation', on the basis that it has often failed to achieve meaningful social change, largely due to a failure to address power imbalances and political realities on the ground (Cooke and Kothari 2001). However, these debates, and the subsequent theoretical and methodological advances, do not seem to have been much applied to arena of inclusive innovation generally, nor to the establishment and facilitation of IPs specifically. This may be partially due to the fact that IPs have evolved from industrial and commercial settings where issues of participation and empowerment are not necessarily a concern.

A fundamental assumption behind the IP approach is that the 'innovation system' in question is not working effectively and that actors within the system need an initial push or opportunity to engage in joint discussion, action, sharing and learning. However, even if IPs succeed in creating a shared forum, they may fail to address the underlying issues which cause weak actor linkages in the first place. Power dynamics can be identified as a key factor governing the nature of interactions between stakeholders. Agricultural IPs bring less powerful actors, such as farmers, together with more influential actors, such as government officers or traders. In theory, platforms enable the members to articulate their needs and work together to achieve a common goal on equal terms. In reality, the goals, interests and perspectives of actors are likely to diverge and may be even in conflict with one another. Achieving consensus can be difficult and sometimes unlikely. Thus, platforms need to find ways of enabling less powerful actors to influence decision-making; a key tenet of inclusivity.

Various works have touched on the issue of power dynamics within platforms. Steins and Edwards (1999) focus on power dynamics and stakeholder representation within platforms on resource use in complex common-pool resource management scenarios. They highlight the importance of empowering platform participants in order to challenge inequalities and dominant power relations. Faysse (2006) describes a number of challenges involved in establishing multi-stakeholder platforms within unfavourable contexts, and asymmetries of power emerge as a key issue in the selected case studies. Faysse, therefore, argues that platforms provide an imperfect negotiation process. Cornwall (2002) also highlights that spaces for citizen participation are not neutral, but are shaped by power relations; and supporting inclusive participation of citizens

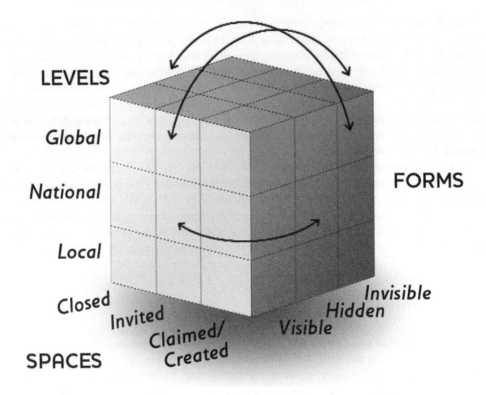

Figure 1. The 'power cube': the levels, spaces and forms of power (Gaventa 2006).

in decision-making arenas calls for greater understanding of the micro-politics of participation as situated practice. Edmunds and Wollenberg (2002) examine the impact of multi-stakeholder platforms for disadvantaged groups and argue that they often mask abuses of power and more structural and enduring inequity. These works indicate that dealing with power dynamics is critical if IPs are to be successful mechanisms for inclusive innovation. However, power dynamics are complex and multi-faceted and vary depending on the context, presenting a challenge for facilitators. There is, therefore, a need for analytical frameworks and tools that can be used to identify these dynamics and investigate their influence on platform processes.

This paper uses the power cube, developed by Gaventa (2006), to critically analyse the IPs used in the Nile Basin Development Challenge. The framework – which has been used as a tool for practitioner reflection – was developed as a means for understanding the ways in which power operates, particularly within spaces which aim to increase citizen engagement in policy processes. The power cube enables important questions to be asked such as: Do new mechanisms for engagement, such as IPs, represent real shifts in power? Do they open up spaces where participation and citizen voice can have an influence? Will increased engagement in platforms risk simply re-legitimizing the status quo, or will it contribute to transforming patterns of exclusion and to challenging power relationships (Gaventa 2006, 23)? The framework (Figure 1) outlines three dimensions of power:

- spaces which refers to the potential arenas for participation and action including closed, invited and claimed spaces;
- forms which refers to the ways in which power manifests itself including its visible, hidden and invisible forms and

- levels which refers to the differing layers of decision-making and authority, including the local, national and global.

The framework highlights that these dimensions are not fixed or static and are constantly inter-relating with each other. The three dimensions are used to organize the paper and are explained in greater detail in Section 5.

3. Research methods

The NBDC project formed district-level IPs in three study sites in the Blue Nile Basin in Ethiopia: Fogera district in Amhara Regional State, and Diga and Jeldu districts in Oromia Regional State. The platforms began in 2011 and are ongoing at the time of writing. We synthesize lessons from the initial phase of platform operationalization. Our analysis is based on the data collected using a mixed method approach.

Prior to IP establishment, 45 farmer focus group discussions were conducted to gather information about NRM planning and implementation processes: three focus groups – male, female and mixed sex – were organized in five research kebeles[2] per woreda.[3] Fifteen to 20 farmers were involved per focus group and included individuals from wealthy, poor and landless households. Kebeles were selected to represent different elevations and cropping systems within the woredas. Researchers also undertook community mapping exercises, transect walks and historical timelines in each kebele and held in-depth interviews with extension agents, district and regional agricultural experts, government administrators and national researchers.

After platforms had been established, participatory community engagement exercises were carried out in three kebeles in each woreda to identify and prioritize community NRM issues. A total of 48 farmers were involved in this process per woreda, 16 farmers per kebele (eight males and eight females). Approximately 10 official IP meetings were held in each site between 2011 and 2013 involving 20–30 people per meeting (platform membership is discussed in more detail in Section 5.2.1). Minutes were recorded for each meeting and stakeholder feedback was documented by NBDC researchers using a combination of semi-structured questionnaires, comment cards and group discussions. In addition to official minutes, researchers recorded their observations of the platform process and pilot interventions.

From 2012 to 2013, each platform undertook pilot interventions in selected kebeles within the study woredas. The interventions were evaluated by platform members and researchers at the end of each season and reports produced. An independent mid-term review of the platforms was conducted between October and December 2012, which involved a review of secondary data, focus group discussions and key informant interviews with platform members, members of the IP technical groups, participant and non-participant farmers.

The authors of this paper were all involved as researchers in the NBDC project and several of the authors were involved in the establishment and facilitation of the IPs. Researcher reflections were critical for documenting platform activities, as well as capturing unspoken or tacit knowledge of the process and the often complex dynamics between stakeholders. It should be highlighted that due to the sensitive political context much of our evidence was generated through informal conversations as much as formal interviews.

4. Ethiopian context

It is important to outline the context within which the platforms are operating. Ethiopia is often cited as an example of severe natural resource degradation. Various land and water management programmes have been implemented on farms and community lands over the past four decades, undertaken by government agencies in collaboration with national and international organizations. However, these have mostly been top-down in nature and failed to take into account the needs, aspirations, constraints and livelihood realities of farming communities (Hoben 1996; Pankhurst 2001; Merrey & Gebreselassie 2011; Ludi et al. 2013). More bottom-up approaches are deemed essential if NRM interventions are to be owned by farmers, be sustainable, and make a meaningful contribution to improved environmental management and livelihoods.

Recently, attempts have been made to incorporate participatory approaches into NRM planning and implementation, with some successes. However, government in Ethiopia is extremely strong and maintains tight control of local decisions, despite formal decentralization; a situation which has persisted since the Derg regime of the 1970s and 1980s. Hagmann and Abbink observe that, 'Although formally a federation, Ethiopia's central power holders keep a tight leash on sub-national entities', and that 'despite its participatory rhetoric ... development is state-centred and state-driven' (2011, 584–585). As a result, there is a contradiction between national plans and output targets which generally take a top-down approach, and attempts to devolve and decentralize planning processes using a participatory approach to the lowest administrative levels. Local government officials have very little experience of stakeholder consultation, locally tailored planning or other cornerstones of innovation. In addition to the political environment, planning and implementation processes are not sufficiently coordinated and institutional structures are often weak with little or no contact between stakeholders. Other challenges include a lack of bottom-up farmer organization, poorly developed markets, poor infrastructure, limited access to information and inadequate extension. As a result, the overall success of NRM interventions to date has been limited.

In recognition of these challenges, IPs were initiated to stimulate new approaches, with particular emphasis on changing the relationships and interactions between stakeholders. However, the Ethiopian institutional and political context proved to be a challenging environment for this model of inclusive innovation. There has been much debate about whether and to what extent external agents can bring about change in such environments through the use of multi-stakeholder processes. Faysse (2006, 220) notes that the nature of the state significantly affects the prospects of successful multi-stakeholder processes; a state which is 'either too strong or too weak to support a multi-stakeholder platform process and decisions' creates an unfavourable environment for such approaches. In order to monitor the platforms' effectiveness, it was critical to understand the nature of stakeholder interactions; the impact of these dynamics on platform activities and to reflect on the extent to which platforms were able to shift these dynamics.

5.   Results and discussion

The three dimensions of the power cube, as described in Section 2, are used as an organizing framework for our analysis. First, we define IPs as *spaces* for participation, and examine who created these spaces, who was invited to participate, who controlled the space and the quality of participation within the space. In order to then understand the *forms* of power operating within the platforms, we analyse who participates and who is excluded, who makes decisions, who implements decisions and who benefits and loses from these actions. Finally, we look at how the local-level platforms relate to the different *levels* of power in the Ethiopian context and how actors and policies at local, regional and national levels influence the platform process. We also explore whether or not platforms could influence higher political levels. Site-specific details of the 'spaces', 'forms' and 'levels' of power are not always discussed below, as our analysis aggregates what we identified as similar patterns across the three platforms. These similarities may partly be due to the project approach as well as the uniformity of the Ethiopian NRM planning and implementation process.

5.1. *IPs as spaces for participation*

'Space' refers to decision-making arenas and forums for action; in this case, the IPs themselves. Power shapes the boundaries of spaces, who may enter them and what is possible within them. The power cube refers to three kinds of spaces: 'closed' spaces which are controlled by a powerful group and difficult or impossible for outsiders to influence; 'invited' spaces where policy-makers invite outsiders to contribute their views to decision-making, allowing influence but within boundaries determined by the powerful and 'claimed' spaces where the less powerful can 'develop their agendas and create solidarity without control from power holders' (Luttrell and Quiroz 2009, 11). Previous studies as well as extensive situational analysis (Merrey and Gebreselassie 2011; Ludi et al. 2013; Snyder et al., 2014) indicate that that local NRM planning and implementation in Ethiopia is a 'closed' or at most nominally 'invited' space. One goal of the NBDC IPs was to create a genuinely invited space where a range of participants could influence how higher level NRM strategies were implemented in their locality, for example, the location, design and timing of interventions.

Who creates the space is critical to who has power within the space and which agendas are pursued. Therefore, an analysis of power and its expression in IPs cannot ignore the role of NBDC researchers. The IPs were instigated by the NBDC project to work on improved NRM. Thus, the agenda of NRM came from researchers, not from district staff or communities. NBDC staff also held visible power as resource providers, without which the platforms would not function. Researchers undertook a situational analysis in all three study sites before the platforms were established. They identified the predominance of top-down approaches to the implementation and the lack of sectoral integration and community participation as major challenges to successful NRM. NBDC researchers proposed IPs as a potential mechanism for dealing with these issues. During initial platform meetings, researchers explained the IP concept and the NBDC research agenda, and shared the results of the situational analysis and perceived challenges. Despite researcher efforts to ensure that IP members understood the aims and objectives of the platforms, often platform participants had a limited understanding of the concepts driving the platform work. This shortcoming may have been due to the fact that the challenges and proposed solutions were largely identified by researchers who analysed the system from an external perspective.

Variations in understanding meant that different actors within the platforms interpreted the platform aims in different ways and used the space to push their own agendas. For example, due to the synergies between the government soil water conservation agenda and the NRM focus of the NBDC research, government workers saw the platforms as an opportunity for achieving government targets. The need for external support in the area of NRM was frequently mentioned by government actors in early platform meetings and it was clear that local government agents were concerned about meeting targets set by regional- and national-level decision-makers. Their interest in the platforms could, therefore, be seen as an attempt to appropriate the platform space for their own purposes in order to capitalize on external expertise. In addition, researchers from the wider NBDC team also sought to utilize the IPs as vehicles for disseminating their research findings. Thus, while platforms focused on issues that were relevant to certain stakeholders, the platforms also presented an opportunity for dominant actors to achieve their goals.

NBDC researchers undertook the initial platform facilitation, including establishing the time and place of platform meetings, giving them a certain degree of control over the process. In addition to researcher facilitation, IP members were encouraged to establish technical committees for the implementation of pilot interventions. These included a range of IP members but were primarily led by government actors. Concerns about ownership and sustainability led NBDC researchers to hand over facilitation to local actors after a year. The process of devolving facilitation was not straightforward. NBDC researchers decided not to transfer facilitation to dominant local government actors – another example of the influence that researchers had over the platform process – and instead local NGOs were assigned due to their more 'neutral' role. However, NGO representatives still had to seek approval from and work alongside local government and in some cases struggled with facilitation capacity. This illustrates the difficulties that 'insiders' may face in navigating power dynamics, particularly if they are part of existing power structures. So although the NBDC platforms succeeded in establishing 'invited' spaces for decision-making, these spaces still operated within boundaries set by more powerful actors, namely project partners and local government. On reflection, creation of truly inclusive 'claimed' spaces for innovation may be unrealistic in a short time period in such a challenging context.

5.2. *Forms of power within the platform space*

It is important to look not only at the spaces for engagement and how they are constructed and managed, but also at what goes on inside them. The power cube outlines three forms of power: visible, hidden and invisible forms. Visible power refers to the observable aspects of decision-making which usually take place in public. It is possible to identify visible signs of power by looking at who participates and who gains and loses within decision-making arenas. However, often little attention is paid to hidden forms of power which refers to the ways in which powerful actors and institutions maintain their power and privilege (cf. Scott 1985). This can include deciding who participates in decision-making and what gets onto the agenda by excluding certain issues from discussion or controlling politics behind the scenes. Hidden forms of power also make certain voices or issues more important than others; this can be based on factors such as gender, age, ethnicity or expertise. Invisible power goes a step further and refers to the social and political culture which shapes the psychological and ideological boundaries of participation. This form of power serves to keep significant issues and problems away from the decision-making arena by influencing how individuals think about their place in the world; for example, their beliefs, sense of self and acceptance of the status quo (Gaventa 2006, 29). These forms of power can, therefore, be much harder to identify and describe.

5.2.1. *Platform membership and representation*

Researchers played a significant role in determining initial platform membership. Due to the project aims, they focused on identifying stakeholders whose mandate was to address NRM issues and who had decision-making power over resources. These included: community representatives, district administrators, government experts from the Bureau of Agriculture, extension agents, national agricultural research centres (NARs), local universities and NGOs. Representatives from these stakeholder groups were invited to an inception meeting which consisted of roughly 12 government staff including extension agents, 4 NBDC researchers, 3 community representatives, 2 NARs researchers, 1 university researcher and 1 NGO representative. The numbers and composition fluctuated in subsequent meetings, but the dominance of government representatives persisted throughout, both in terms of numbers and the degree of power that these participants were able to exert on the process. The dominance of local government was also established very visibly in all three sites by the fact that platform meetings were held in woreda offices.

Stakeholder analysis before platform inception indicated public sector dominance of NRM, a lack of civil society actors and the weak role of the private sector. To some extent, this lack of diversity among actors may reflect the NRM focus of the research. However, an investigation of Ethiopian rural innovation systems and networks conducted by Spielman et al. (2010) also found that government extension and administration exert a strong influence over smallholder networks, crowding out market-based and civil society actors thereby limiting innovation processes. The dominance of certain stakeholders is an important consideration for IPs. This has been alluded to by Wennink and Ochola (2011), who state that government actors must be treated like any other platform members. However, this is not always achievable. Although NBDC researchers were aware of the potential power that government representatives could exert on the process, they were unable to take steps to ensure more balanced representation of stakeholders. This was partly due to the lack of diversity in the Ethiopian institutional context, but also due to the fact that government endorsement was a prerequisite for the project to become operational, and this included stakeholder selection.

In the NBDC platforms, the power of local government representatives was particularly visible in the selection of 'community representatives'. In all three sites, it was decided that a kebele chairman or manager should participate in platform meetings, ideally alongside one or more community representatives. Kebele leaders work for the government at local level and act as intermediaries between the government and the wider community. Farmer representatives were selected according to certain criteria: they should be active, able to represent other farmers and report outcomes of meetings to the wider community. As a result those selected were often 'model farmers' who were handpicked by the district administration. Model farmers play a prominent role in the local administrative structure and are expected to persuade their neighbours to support government initiatives and to participate in developmental activities (Williamson 2011). The selection process for model farmers is also subject to local power dynamics. Research has found that such farmers are often selected by local leaders based on relationships and political patronage rather than on their knowledge, farming abilities and willingness to assist others (Lemma and Hoffmann 2005). It is, therefore, likely that both the kebele leaders and the selected 'farmer representatives' who were invited to platform meetings were supportive of government agendas and not necessarily representative of the wider community.

The 'farmer representative' selection process within the platforms can be seen as an example of false homogenization as outlined by Luttrell and Quiroz (2009), when stakeholders are grouped, and hence represented in ways which do not reflect their true diversity. NBDC researchers found it difficult to challenge the selection of farmer representatives as too much interference risked derailing the process. This meant that in reality, researchers had limited power over platform composition. The issue of who has control over stakeholder representation has important implications for IPs, particularly if they are established to encourage the participation and innovative capacity of the poor. The consequences of who is represented and who is excluded can be demonstrated when looking at the decisions and subsequent interventions undertaken by the NBDC platforms.

5.2.2. Decision-making

The starting point for each platform was the identification of a commonly agreed upon NRM issue. In Diga, the issue of land degradation was selected; in Fogera, unrestricted grazing was chosen and in Jeldu, soil erosion. Although these issues were evidently important for platform members, NBDC researchers suspected that the choice of these entry points was significantly influenced by a large-scale government Sustainable Land Management (SLM) campaign that was taking place throughout Ethiopia at the time. Due to concerns about dominant government interests and a lack of community representation in the prioritization of key issues, a series of 'community engagement' exercises were conducted in selected kebeles in each district. These exercises revealed significant differences in the prioritization of NRM issues between farmers and decision-makers. Farmer-selected issues, although linked to land degradation, were more focused on immediate livelihood concerns. They included termite infestation, crop disease, water shortage and lack of livestock feed. In contrast, issues selected by decision-makers reflected longer term concerns with landscape-wide soil and water management. While such discrepancies are to be expected, this serves to highlight the ways in which hidden forms of power can be exerted over multi-stakeholder negotiations in order to achieve the objectives of dominant actors. In this case, power was expressed through the influence of government sensitization pro- grammes on the prioritization of key issues.

Conflicting perspectives came to a head when the results of community engagement exercises were presented to the platforms. In Diga, platform members prioritized land degradation rather than the issue of termite infestation identified by farmers from the wider community. In Fogera, although unrestricted grazing was identified as a common issue by members of the plat- form and community members, there were very different views about how this issue should be addressed. Government representatives wanted to take immediate action by confining livestock to homesteads, whereas farmers thought it should be tackled over a longer time frame through a range of interventions, partly due to concerns about producing sufficient fodder. In Jeldu, there was apparent consensus between members of the community and the platform members who both prioritized soil erosion, but this may have been because NBDC community engagement exercises coincided with the government SLM campaign, which entailed 'awareness raising' activities in every kebele of participating districts.

The selection of NRM issues was a critical point in the IP process as these issues were used to identify entry points for interventions. Although there was a lack of consensus regarding the issues, platform members in all three sites decided to focus on fodder interventions as a way of meeting both the short-term needs of farmers and the longer term goals of decision-makers. This was largely due to researchers from the International Livestock Research Institute (ILRI) who played a key mediating role. In Diga, researchers identified a termite-resistant fodder grass that could provide livestock feed and rehabilitate degraded land. In Fogera, improved forage production was seen as a way of enabling farmers to meet their livestock's fodder needs and control grazing. In Jeldu, fodder interventions were seen as a way to increase livestock feed and improve soil and water conservation. While this highlights the contribution that external facilitators can make if they have an overview of the context and are able to highlight synergies between apparently conflicting perspectives, the fact that fodder interventions were pursued in all three sites cannot be ignored and illustrates another sphere of influence over the process.

Much has been written about the influence that donor organizations unwittingly have over 'participatory' selection processes. Described as the 'development effect', participants frame their needs in terms of what they know or assume that the implementing agency will be able to deliver, thereby securing 'known benefits' (Mosse 2001). Critiques of participation also high- light that researchers and development practitioners often use participatory approaches to achieve their own agendas or those of their organizations. In this case, it seems that the promotion of fodder interventions was not a conscious ploy by ILRI researchers but rather researchers drawing on their own knowledge and experience, which was limited to a certain area of expertise. Fodder interventions were in many ways a compromise between farmer and decision-maker inter- ests, so to an extent the interventions met the demands of both groups. However, it is possible that it was easier for platform participants to mirror the discourse and preferred solutions of the 'experts', in this case, the researchers facilitating the platforms than making more complex and differentiated statements of preferences (Cornwall 2004, 84).

5.2.3. *Implementation*

The next step was to design innovative interventions. Due to the need to meet certain project objectives, NBDC researchers again influenced this process by stressing that piloting should permit exploration of the factors influencing adoption and effectiveness of the innovations. Three different approaches were, therefore, applied in each site: backyard fodder development by individuals at household level; planting of fodder on soil and water conservation structures and area enclosure of communal grazing areas. Improved forages were then chosen by experts to suit local agro-ecologies. After the innovations had been designed, farmers were selected by the woreda (district) Livestock Development Agency in collaboration with extension agents in target kebeles and invited to participate. In the first year, 40 farmers participated in Diga, 13 in Fogera and 96 in Jeldu. One of the selection criteria for participating farmers was that they should express an interest in fodder development. However, during the farmer selection process there was limited consideration for the needs of different types of farmers. Variations in livestock holdings, land size and wealth were not taken into account, and farmers without livestock were not included.

One of the most commonly raised issues in institutionalizing participatory innovation processes is how to incorporate the diverse and often competing needs of participants. Deeper engagement and greater farmer participation in the planning and design of the innovations could have helped rectify this deficiency. However, during the first year of the pilot, farmers were largely seen by IP members as 'implementers' rather than co-designers. As a result in most sites, participating farmers were not aware that the selection and design of the pilot interventions were part of an IP process. This led to different understandings of the innovation process between decision-makers and farmers. Platforms are designed for deliberation, which means that participants should have sufficient knowledge of the aims and objectives of the platform and the theories at work to engage in a meaningful way (Faysse 2006, 225). In the first year of the pilot, community members were not able to discuss or influence the design of innovations due to their exclusion from the process. It is likely that the platforms and the resulting innovations were seen as yet another top-down government programme by participating farmers. As a result, the IP activities reflected and reinforced existing gaps between community members and decision-makers rather than overcoming them.

In Fogera, this gap became apparent when initial interventions were destroyed shortly after activities began; farmers in the first pilot village uprooted the improved fodder plants they themselves had planted. During subsequent investigation by researchers, a number of farmers expressed suspicions that platform interventions were part of an agenda to take communal land for a government afforestation programme. Such perceptions are widespread in Ethiopia due to a history of insecure tenure and land redistribution initiatives under previous regimes. As a result, farmer resistance to NRM innovations is common and presents a significant barrier to the sustainability of NRM initiatives. Community members had not raised these issues with platform members during implementation, and it is debatable whether they would have revealed such concerns to government administrators. Eventually, the platform was forced to abandon activities and establish a new site elsewhere.

This illustrates that although it can be difficult for less powerful actors to influence platform dynamics, they still have significant power to resist innovations through non-engagement. Scott (1985) describes a number of tactics including foot dragging, dissimulation, false compliance, feigned ignorance and sabotage as 'weapons of the weak'. Gaventa (2006) refers to such strategies as hidden forms of power, as they often take place outside formal and public decision-making arenas. Such forms of hidden power illustrate that power dynamics are often more complex than they initially appear and seemingly powerless actors can have more agency than is assumed. These forms of resistance also suggest that although the IPs brought farmers into the decision-making space and nominally involved them in planning and implementation processes, the platforms were not necessarily effective at influencing deep-structure power dynamics influencing stakeholder interactions.

5.2.4. *Interactions between stakeholders*

Even if members of the wider community had been included in the IPs, they would not necessarily have been free to express their points of view. As Hildyard et al. (2001, 69) pointed out, identifying stakeholders and getting them around the table will only create effective dialogue if 'all the actors involved are deemed to have equal bargaining power'. There was a sense that participating farmers were reluctant to express alternative views in platform meetings because these spaces were 'infused with existing relations of power' (Cornwall 2004, 80). Various studies in Ethiopia have observed that opposition or minority views are often not tolerated and can even result in people being denied access to resources (Pausewang, Tronvoll, and Aalen 2002; Aalen and Tronvoll 2009).

In addition to the restrictive political context, widely held negative attitudes towards farmers did not create a conducive environment for farmer participation. In all three platform meetings, decision-makers frequently complained about farmer ignorance of key issues. In early meetings, decision-makers highlighted 'lack of knowledge', 'limited awareness of NRM', 'backward or inappropriate farming practices' and 'farmers' short-term vision' as some of the main challenges to improved NRM. These perceptions have undermined self-confidence among farmers, many of whom seem to have internalized the narratives presented by decision-makers. Farmers participating in platform meetings frequently stated that they 'lacked awareness', thereby reinforcing decision-maker perceptions.

This internalization of government narratives can be seen as an example of invisible power whereby people come to understand their situation as unchangeable or inevitable. Such attitudes and patterns of interaction between community members and decision-makers are intimately related to struggles over resources, governance and power and are often firmly ingrained. Vaughan and Tronvoll (2003a, vi) observe that 'the process of socialization from birth often teaches Ethiopians that people are not equal' which leads to deeply entrenched power relations that cannot easily be changed. The fact that similar patterns emerged in all three platforms, located in different parts of the country, suggests that these dynamics are widespread throughout Ethiopia. These forms of invisible power are important to identify because they have a great deal of influence over platform processes. One of the main aims of IPs is to facilitate knowledge sharing between actors; however, such attitudes inhibit farmers' ability to share their perspectives, knowledge and experiences. This situation represents a major institutional barrier to inclusive innovation and is extremely difficult to address with platform members. Platform facilitators came to realize that platforms may have limited impact in terms of challenging entrenched mind-sets.

5.3. *Levels of power*

Much of this analysis so far has focused on power dynamics at the local level, namely the roles played by NBDC researchers, farmers and local-level decision makers. This focus reflects the research agenda and the fact that interactions between actors at the local level were identified as a critical factor for the success of NRM interventions. However, there is significant debate regarding which level of power is the most important to address. There are some who argue that changing power dynamics must begin locally, while others argue that the nation state is still the main source of power and public authority. The power cube recognizes that what is going on at all levels – local, national and global – is potentially significant, as well as the inter-relationships between people working at these levels. During the NBDC IP process, researchers became increasingly aware of the impact of interactions between different levels of power, namely between local-, regional- and national-level actors.

The hierarchical social and political environment in Ethiopia has been cited by a number of studies as an impediment to participatory approaches. As Vaughan and Tronvoll (2003b, 33) write, 'the pattern of social interaction in Ethiopia sustains a strictly hierarchical stratification of society, where one is constrained by a large, invisible, but rigid system of common sanctions, to obey "orders from above"'. Despite rhetoric about decentralization, local government officials are subject to top-down power from higher levels of government which can impede local attempts at participatory, inclusive approaches to planning, innovation and implementation. Ayele (2011, 143) writes that 'local government is not adequately institutionalized to exist as an autonomous level of government ... explicit and implicit provisions in the regional constitutions and statutes render local government a subsidiary structure whose function is limited to implementing centrally adopted policies'. This is expressed in the quota-based NRM implementation framework, and the pressure placed on government staff to meet targets. Hoben (1996, iv) has also written that the 'cumulative effect of top-down attitudes does not support the adoption of a participatory, error-embracing approach to agricultural development'. In this respect, there is often a lack of consideration for the challenges faced by local-level decision-makers in the analysis of power dynamics. Local-level government officials operating within this environment are constrained by higher level decision-making processes at regional level and national level which they have little power to change. They are acutely aware of these dynamics and as such there is a lack of incentive to do things differently; in other words, a lack of incentive for local innovation.

Fiszbein (1997, 3 cited in Ribot 2003, 61) highlights that in some cases, the inability to conduct effective participatory approaches may not be due to a lack of capacity but, rather, poorly designed incentives. Intensive engagement with community members is often difficult to undertake and adds to already strenuous workloads. Local government administrators, therefore, need to see clear advantages of a participatory rather than top-down approach, yet in Ethiopia various structural factors militate against this. Discussions with Jeldu IP members during the first platform meeting revealed that NRM planning is largely top-down because the main priority of local administrators is to fulfil quotas set by national and regional decision-makers. They generally agreed that more bottom-up approaches to NRM planning and implementation could help to better tailor plans to local contexts but they queried whether they would still be able to achieve the ambitious targets outlined by the Government of Ethiopia's Growth and Transformation Plan. Although participatory approaches are outlined in NRM guidelines as part of recent decentralization efforts, in reality they are often not carried out. Authorization and incentives from central government may therefore be required in order to encourage participatory initiatives. Platform members in all three sites questioned why the NBDC project was not focusing attention on communicating these issues to regional- and national-level actors. Certainly, given the importance placed on meeting targets set out in national policy, it is critical for IP facilitators to frame the importance of participatory approaches and of local innovation in reference to these policy goals.

Although local-level IPs can help make these power dynamics visible, they are unlikely to transform them. In this case, it seems that engagement with regional and national actors is required to influence the way things are done at a higher level and on a longer term basis. The NBDC project aims to present evidence generated from the three local case studies to higher level actors through a national-level IP to advocate for change. Other research platforms in Ethiopia have successfully used evidence of local problems and the failure of existing ways of working to strengthen the hand of district officials in negotiating with regional-level authorities (Tucker, Le

Borgne, and Lotti 2013). This approach highlights the potential role that interconnected IPs at multiple levels could play in influencing policy. However, political will is required for changes to take place in addition to evidence that policy changes can support the achievement of national objectives.

6. Conclusion

As the NBDC IPs are ongoing, this paper can only document lessons learned from the initial stages of the platform process. Many of the challenges faced by the NBDC platforms are context specific. Nonetheless, lessons can be drawn and perhaps used to inform other IP processes and other forms of inclusive innovation. Experience from the NBDC platforms demonstrates that power dynamics need to be acknowledged and dealt with explicitly. One of the first steps in dealing with power dynamics is to recognize that IPs are not neutral mechanisms; they aim to promote change which can bring benefits for some but may have negative effects on others. Often these changes fundamentally challenge the existing distribution of power and can thus be threatening to vested interests. The benefits that result from such innovation processes are likely to be determined by who initiates them, who participates and who has influence over the process. If such power dynamics are well understood, then perhaps ways can be found to mediate them, manage potential negative consequences and work for positive change.

In order to identify, analyse and challenge power dynamics, certain tools and frameworks are required. The power cube is one possible approach and highlights the multiple dimensions of power that should be considered. This framework has been useful in conducting a retrospective analysis of the power dynamics in the NBDC IPs, but it may also be applied to other models of inclusive innovation. Our findings illustrate that visible forms of power in particular may be easily identified, whereas hidden and invisible forms are more difficult to uncover and by their nature will be difficult to address. In the case of the NBDC project, it seems that IPs are unlikely to have any significant impact if they merely address visible forms of power at the local level without addressing hidden and invisible power dynamics as well as structural blockages at higher levels. So, although IPs may achieve some short-term successes at local level, significant changes to institutional arrangements and incentive mechanisms may be required at higher levels to make longer lasting change tenable at larger scales. As Gaventa (2006) argues, successful change requires thinking not only about individual dimensions of power but also about how each dimension relates to the other. This multidimensionality is a huge challenge and suggests that in order for meaningful change to take place in inclusive innovation systems then multiple, linked strategies at different levels must be designed that incorporate an appropriate time frame and build the capacity of concerned stakeholders.

Even if IPs cannot solve problems of power and representation, they may serve to make these issues more visible, and can potentially play a role in building people's capacities to change these dynamics (Hiemstra, Brouwer, and van Vugt 2012). However, the degree to which platforms are able to address power dynamics depends largely on how they are facilitated. As Swaans et al. (2013) argue (see also Swaans et al. 2014), the success of such platforms is heavily linked to the attitude, skills and capacities of the facilitator or 'innovation broker'. Identifying and analysing power dynamics and their effects on inclusive innovation demand high levels of reflexivity and awareness. While reflexivity is perhaps possible within a research context, when IPs are mainstreamed as part of development interventions, facilitators may find this challenging.

In summary, those who instigate innovation platform processes need to recognize that altering power dynamics is a complex, difficult and lengthy process. However, if power dynamics are not taken into account in the formulation and facilitation of IPs, there is a danger that platforms give the illusion of increased participation whilst simultaneously replicating and masking existing conditions. It may therefore be necessary to question whether IPs are appropriate mechanisms for achieving inclusive innovation in certain conditions, and whether other models may also need to be considered. This is important to acknowledge because if power imbalances are not adequately addressed such processes may in fact aggravate poverty and environmental decline rather than providing innovative solutions.

Acknowledgements

The authors wish to thank Aberra Adie, Gerba Leta and Elias Damtew for their valuable inputs to this project. We also acknowledge the contribution of Aklilu Amsalu.

Funding

This work was supported by the Challenge Program on Water and Food.

Notes

1. Consultative Group on International Agricultural Research.
2. Administrative unit, equivalent to a neighbourhood.
3. Administrative unit, equivalent to a district.

References

Aalen, L., and K. Tronvoll. 2009. "The End of Democracy? Curtailing Political and Civil Rights in Ethiopia." *Review of African Political Economy* 36 (120): 193–207. doi:10.1080/03056240903065067

Altenburg, T., H. Schmitz, and A. Stamm. 2008. "Breakthrough China's and India's Transition from Production to Innovation." *World Development* 36 (2): 325–344. doi:http://dx.doi.org/10.1016/j.worlddev.2007.06.011

Anderson, J. R., G. Feder, and S. Ganguly. 2006. "The Rise and Fall of Training and Visit Extension: An Asian Mini-drama with an African Epilogue." World Bank Policy Research Working Paper 3928. http://elibrary.worldbank.org/doi/book/10.1596/1813-9450-3928

Ayele, Z. 2011. "Local Government in Ethiopia: Still an Apparatus of Control?" *Law, Democracy and Development* 15: 133–159. doi:http://dx.doi.org/10.4314%2Fldd.v15i1.7

Chambers, R. 1994. "The Origins and Practice of Participatory Rural Appraisal." *World Development* 22 (7): 953–969. http://www.sciencedirect.com/science/article/B6VC6-45F5WRF-5G/2/6c15bb76d4535016f5064da4c1075251

Cooke, B., and U. Kothari, eds. 2001. *Participation: The New Tyranny?* London: Zed Books.

Cornwall, A. 2002. "Making Spaces, Changing Places: Situating Participation in Development." IDS Working Paper 170. http://www.drc-citizenship.org/system/assets/1052734369/original/1052734369-cornwall.2002-making.pdf?1289311080

Cornwall, A. 2004. "Spaces for Transformation? Reflections on Issues of Power and Difference in Participation in Development." In *Participation: From Tyranny to Transformation? Exploring New Approaches to Participation in Development*, edited by S. Hickey, and G. Mohan, 75–91. London: Zed Books.

Edmunds, D., and E. Wollenberg. 2002. "Disadvantaged Groups in Multistakeholder Negotiations." CIFOR Programme Report. http://www.cifor.org/publications/pdf_files/Strategic_Negotiation_report.pdf

Faysse, N. 2006. "Troubles on the Way: An Analysis of the Challenges Faced by Multi-Stakeholder Platforms." *United Nations Sustainable Development Journal* 30 (3): 219–229. doi:10.1111/j.1477-8947.2006.00112.x

Fiszbein, A. 1997. "Decentralization and Local Capacity: Some Thoughts on a Controversial Relationship." Paper presented at the FAO/UNCDF/World Bank Technical Consultation on Decentralization, Rome, December 15–18.

Gaventa, J. 2006. "Finding the Spaces for Change: A Power Analysis." *IDS Bulletin* 37 (6): 23–33. doi:10.1111/j.1759-5436.2006.tb00320.x

Hagmann, T., and J. Abbink. 2011. "Twenty Years of Revolutionary Democratic Ethiopia, 1991 to 2011." *Journal of Eastern African Studies* 5 (4): 579–595. doi:http://dx.doi.org/DOI:10.1080/17531055.2011.642515

Hall, A., G. Bockett, S. Taylor, M. V. K. Sivamohan, and N. Clark. 2001. "Why Research Partnerships Really Matter: Innovation Theory, Institutional Arrangements and Implications for Developing New Technology for the Poor." *World Development* 29 (5): 783–797. doi:http://dx.doi.org/10.1016/S0305-750X(01)00004-3

Hall, A., W. Janssen, E. Pehu, and R. Rajalahti. 2006. *Enhancing Agricultural Innovation: How to go Beyond the Strengthening of Research Systems*. Washington, DC: World Bank. http://siteresources.worldbank.org/INTARD/Resources/Enhancing_Ag_Innovation.pdf

Hiemstra, W., H. Brouwer, and S. van Vugt. 2012. *Power Dynamics in Multi-Stakeholder Processes: A Balancing Act*. Wageningen: Wageningen UR Centre for Development Innovation with partners. http://www.wageningenur.nl/en/Publication-details.htm?publicationId=publication-way-343332333739

Hildyard, N., P. Hegde, P. Wolvekamp, and S. Redyy. 2001. "Pluralism, Participation and Power: Joint Forest Management in India." In *Participation: The New Tyranny?*, edited by B. Cooke and U. Kothari, 56–71. London: Zed Books.

Hoben, A. 1996. "Land Tenure Policy in Ethiopia: Issues for Smallholder Sustainable Agricultural Growth." Report prepared for World Bank, Washington DC.

Klerkx, L., B. van Mierlo, and C. Leeuwis. 2012. "Evolution of Systems Approaches to Agricultural Innovations: Concepts, Analysis and Interventions." In *Farming Systems Research into the 21st Century: The New Dynamic*, edited by I. Darnhofer, D. Gibbon, and B. Dedieu, 457–483. Dordrecht: Springer. http://www.academia.edu/1569316/Evolution_of_systems_approaches_to_agricultural_innovation_Concepts_analysis_and_interventions

Lemma, M., and V. Hoffmann. 2005. "The Agricultural Knowledge System in Tigray, Ethiopia: Empirical Study about its Recent History and Actual Effectiveness." Conference on international agricultural research for development, Stuttgart, Hohenheim. http://www.tropentag.de/2005/abstracts/full/49.pdf

Ludi, E., A. Belay, A. Duncan, K. Snyder, J. Tucker, B. Cullen, M. Belissa, et al. 2013. *Rhetoric versus Realities: A Diagnosis of Rainwater Management Development Processes in the Blue Nile Basin of Ethiopia*. Colombo, Sri Lanka: CGIAR Challenge Program on Water and Food (CPWF). 58P [CPWF Research for Development (R4D) Series 5]. http://cgspace.cgiar.org/bitstream/handle/10568/27603/cpwf_r4d5.pdf?sequence=1

Lundvall, B. A. 1992. *National Systems of Innovation. Towards a Theory of Innovation and Interactive Learning*. London: Pinter.

Luttrell, C., and S. Quiroz. 2009. "Understanding and Operationalising Empowerment." ODI Working Paper 308. ODI, London. http://www.odi.org.uk/sites/odi.org.uk/files/odi-assets/publications-opinion-files/5500.pdf

Merrey, D. J., and T. Gebreselassie. 2011. "Promoting Improved Rainwater and Land Management in the Blue Nile (Abay) Basin of Ethiopia." NBDC Technical Report 1.2 vols. Nairobi, Kenya, ILRI. http://cgspace.cgiar.org/handle/10568/3317

Mosse, D. 2001. "'Peoples Knowledge', Participation and Patronage: Operations and Representations in Rural Development." In *Participation: The New Tyranny?*, edited by B. Cooke and U. Kothari, 16–35. London: Zed Books.

Nederlof, S., M. Wongtschowski, and F. van der Lee, eds. 2011. *Putting Heads Together: Agricultural Innovation Platforms in Practice. Bulletin 396*. Amsterdam: KIT Publishers. http://www.kitpublishers.nl/net/KIT_Publicaties_output/showfile.aspx?e=1953

Pankhurst, A., ed. 2001. *Natural Resource Management in Ethiopia*. Ethiopia: Forum for Social Studies.

Pausewang, S., K. Tronvoll, and L. Aalen, eds. 2002. *Ethiopia Since the Derg: A Decade of Democratic Pretension and Performance*. London: Zed Books.

Ribot, J. C. 2003. "Democratic Decentralization of Natural Resources: Institutional Choice and Discretionary Power Transfers in Sub-Saharan Africa." *Public Administration and Development* 23 (1): 53–65. doi:10.1002/pad.259

Scott, J. C. 1985. *Weapons of the Weak: Everyday Forms of Peasant Resistance*. New Haven: Yale University Press.

Snyder, K., E. Ludi, B. Cullen, J. Tucker, A. Belay, and A. Duncan. 2014. "Participation and Performance: Decentralised Planning and Implementation in Ethiopia." *Public Administration and Development* 34 (4): 83–95. doi:10.1002/pad.1680

Spielman, D. J. 2005. "Innovation Systems Perspective on Developing-Country Agriculture: A Critical Review." ISNAR Discussion Paper No. 2 (IFPRI). http://ageconsearch.umn.edu/bitstream/59692/2/isnardp02.pdf

Spielman, D., K. Davis, M. Negash, and G. Ayele. 2010. "Rural Innovation Systems and Networks: Findings from a Study of Ethiopian Smallholders." *Agriculture and Human Values* 28 (2): 195–212. doi:10.1007/s10460-010-9273-y

Steins, N. A., & V. M. Edwards. 1999. "Synthesis: Platforms for Collective Action in Multiple-Use Common-Pool Resources." *Agriculture and Human Values* 16 (3): 309–315. doi:10.1023/A:1007587330755

Swaans, K., B. Cullen, A. van Rooyen, A. Adekunle, H. Ngwenya, Z. Lemma, and S. Nederlof. 2013. "Dealing with Critical Challenges in Innovation Platforms: Lessons for Facilitation." *Knowledge Management for Development* 9 (3): 116–135. http://journal.km4dev.org/index.php/km4dj/article/viewFile/154/267

Swaans, K., B. Boogaard, R. Bendapudi, H. Taye, S. Hendrickx, and L. Klerkx. 2014. "Operationalising Inclusive Innovation: Lessons from Innovation Platforms in Livestock Value Chains in India and Mozambique." *Innovation and Development* 4 (2): 239–257. doi: 10.1080/2157930X.2014.925246

Tucker, J., E. Le Borgne, and M. Lotti. 2013. "Policy and Practice Influence through Research: Critical Reflections on RiPPLE's Approach." In *Achieving Water Security: Lessons from Research in Water Supply, Sanitation and Hygiene in Ethiopia*, edited by I. R. Calow, E. Ludi, and J. Tucker, 173–192. Practical Action: Rugby.

Vaughan, S., and K. Tronvoll. 2003a. "Structures and Relations of Power." Ethiopia. Background Document prepared for Sida's Country Strategy 2003–2007.

Vaughan, S., and K. Tronvoll. 2003b. "The Culture of Power in Contemporary Ethiopian Political Life." *SIA Studies* 10. http://www.sida.se/Publications/Import/pdf/sv/The-Culture-of-Power-in-Contemporary-Ethiopian-Political-Life.pdf

Wennink, B., and W. Ochola. 2011. "Designing Innovation Platforms." In *Putting Heads Together: Agricultural Innovation Platforms in Practice*, edited by S. Nederlof, M. Wongtschowski, and F. van der Lee, 30–42. Bulletin 396. Amsterdam: KIT Publishers. http://www.kitpublishers.nl/net/KIT_Publicaties_output/showfile.aspx?e=1953

Williamson, V. 2011. "So Near and Yet so Far: Values and Mental Models Along the Aid Chain in Ethiopia." *Journal of International Development* 23 (6): 823–835. doi:10.1002/jid.1812

When grassroots innovation movements encounter mainstream institutions: implications for models of inclusive innovation

Mariano Fressoli[a], Elisa Arond[b], Dinesh Abrol[c], Adrian Smith[d], Adrian Ely[d] and Rafael Dias[e]

[a]Instituto de Estudios sobre la Ciencia y la Tecnología, Universidad Nacional de Quilmes – CONICET, Argentina; [b]Graduate School of Geography, Clark University, USA; [c]Centre for Studies in Science Policy, Jawaharlal Nehru University, New Delhi, India; [d]SPRU, University of Sussex, UK; [e]Grupo de Análise de Políticas de Inovação, Limeira, Brazil

Grassroots innovation movements (GIMs) can be regarded as initiators or advocates of alternative pathways of innovation. Sometimes these movements engage with more established science, technology and innovation (STI) institutions and development agencies in pursuit of their goals. In this paper, we argue that an important aspect to encounters between GIMs and mainstream STI institutions is the negotiation of different framings of grassroots innovation and development of policy models for inclusive innovation. These encounters can result in two different modes of engagement by GIMs; what we call *insertion* and *mobilization*. We illustrate and discuss these interrelated notions of framings and modes of engagement by drawing on three case studies of GIMs: the Social Technologies Network in Brazil, and the Honey Bee Network and People's Science Movements in India. The cases highlight that inclusion in the context of GIMs is not an unproblematic, smooth endeavour, and involves diverse interpretations and framings, which shape what and who gets included or excluded. Within the context of increasing policy interest, the analysis of encounters between GIMs and STI institutions can offer important lessons for the design of models of inclusive innovation and development.

1. Introduction

Grassroots innovation involves movements and networks of academics, activists and practitioners who seek to experiment with alternative forms of knowledge creation and processes for innovation. These alternatives harness local ingenuity directed towards local development. Grassroots innovation can be aimed at fostering inclusion as a process (e.g. fostering participation in the design of technology), as an outcome (e.g. providing services for marginalized groups), or even endeavour to produce structural change (e.g. enabling broad and diverse participation in the shaping and priority-setting of policies and institutions oriented to promoting science, technology and innovation, STI).

Historical examples of grassroots innovation movements (GIMs) include, among others, the Appropriate Technology movement in the 1960s and 1970s, the Lucas Plan and movement for socially useful production in the UK, and the Alternative Technology movement (Smith 2005). Many of these activities were subsequently supported (often at an early phase) by development agencies and science and technology institutions. For instance, sections of the OECD and International Labour Organisation, as well as the World Bank, UNDP, UNEP and several Science and Technology institutions at the national level, conducted activities around 'appropriate technology' in the 1970s and 1980s. So, development agencies and mainstream Science and Technology institutions have historically shown interest in alternative models of technological change and social development originating in GIMs.

With the impact of the current global economic crisis, new political attention to issues of inequality and social inclusion has drawn institutional attention once more to GIMs and varied notions of inclusive innovation. For example, the OECD has started to develop concepts and models of intervention around 'inclusive innovation', 'inclusive growth' and 'inclusive development' (see de Mello and Dutz 2012; OECD 2012a; OECD 2012b, respectively). This activity includes recognition of grassroots innovation, as well as 'bottom of the pyramid' (Prahalad 2005) and 'frugal' innovation (Bound and Thornton 2012) models. Other examples of interest on the part of international development agencies include the World Bank (Utz and Dahlman 2007), and the United Nations Development Programme (UNDP 2010, 2013), among others. Thus, within the context of increasing interest in inclusive models of innovation, it is important to realize that though inclusion is a fashionable word at the moment, it involves a diversity of interpretations and ways of framing what gets included, and what remains excluded. Therefore, it is relevant to analyse how policies and programmes at national and international levels are engaging with ongoing, vibrant GIMs in different country contexts.

In this paper, we aim to study how GIM encounters with mainstream institutions of STI can lead to the development of new models of inclusive innovation. We analyse how different framings and interpretations of innovation, social inclusion and participation are negotiated and contested, and what modes of engagement GIMs use in order to forge alternative pathways of innovation (Hess 2007; Smith 2007). In order to do this, we focus on selected encounters experienced by specific grassroots innovation social movements: the Social Technologies Network (STN) in Brazil, the People's Science Movements (PSM) and the Honey Bee Network (HBN) in India. The approaches, experiences and encounters with mainstream STI institutions are different in each case. We consider some of the events, issues and arenas where encounters with mainstream innovation have been particularly pronounced.

Our analysis consequently uses the varied experiences in these cases to explore how policy interest in 'models' relates to the plurality of ideas, approaches and contexts of grassroots movements, which are focused on building locally sensitive alternative pathways for grassroots innovation. Further, the cases highlight that inclusion is not an unproblematic, smooth endeavour; rather, in practice it can also involve uneven, unequal, incomplete and sometimes antagonistic processes and outcomes. We argue that the analysis of encounters between GIMs and mainstream STI institutions can offer important lessons for the design of models of inclusive innovation and development around the world.

The paper is structured as follows. The following section builds on prior work on social movement framings of grassroots innovation to discuss models of grassroots or inclusive innovation, as well as two different 'modes of engagement' that shape GIM encounters with mainstream STI institutions. Section 3 presents the three GIM cases and their 'encounters' with mainstream innovation and development institutions and policies. Section 4 presents some analysis of the three cases' experiences, and related discussion. The conclusion offers some lessons for policymakers' intent on building models of inclusive innovation.

2. From framings to models: insertion and mobilization

Current interest in inclusive innovation has fostered interactions between GIMs and mainstream STI institutions. Encounters with mainstream STI institutions are often important for the survival and expansion of grassroots innovation, for example, by providing resources and/or scaling up experiences. But such encounters can also be controversial since mainstream systems of innovation and GIMs usually rely on different approaches to innovation which might generate an uneasy mix of cooperation and competition for ideas and models of innovation for development. Thus, although STI and GIM are neither clear-cut nor antagonistic positions, it is important to consider what their differences are in their approach to innovation (see Table 1 based on Ely et al. 2013).

As Letty, Shezi, and Mudhara (2012, 1) point out, it is common to associate grassroots innovation with the general aim of 'exercising control over the innovation process' as well as participation in the design of technologies, policies and regulations, thus regarding grassroots innovation as distinct from mainstream STI. However, while a strict definition casts grassroots innovation as innovation coming *from* the 'grassroots' (Gupta 2013) (meaning that it is generally a result of a bottom-up process emanating from communities and users), in practice it can also include actions *with* and *by* governments, R&D institutions and aid agencies directed to and including marginalized groups (see Cozzens and Sutz 2012).

On the other hand, mainstream systems of STI are often associated with relatively centralized, formally organized research institutions. Innovation policy aims are generally expressed as an imperative to catch-up with or keep-up with an apparently universal techno-economic frontier, typically based on information technology, biotechnology and nanotechnology (Freeman 1992;

Table 1. Mainstream STI institutions and GIMs' approaches to innovation.

Characteristics	Mainstream STI	GIMs
Political dimensions		
Predominant actors	Universities, public labs, commercial firms, ministries and other public institutions, international funding agencies	Civil society, NGOs, social movements, cooperatives
Priority values	Scientific advance, for-profit innovation/not necessarily focused on social inclusion	Social justice/not necessarily focused on for-profit innovation
Mechanisms		
Principal incentives/ drivers	Market demand and regulation/science competence	Social needs/cooperation and community empowerment
Sources of investment	State/corporate funded, venture capital	Development aid, community finance, donations, state funding
Forms of appropriability	Intellectual property framework strongly biased towards patent-based innovation	Not appropriated by individuals – seen as common goods
Knowledge dimensions		
Sites of innovation	Laboratories and R&D institutes, boardrooms and ministries, market-based firms	Community projects and participatory processes, social movements
Predominant forms of knowledge	Scientific and technical knowledge	Local, situated knowledge/ indigenous knowledge
Emblematic technological fields	Biotechnology, ICTs, nanotechnology	Organic food, small-scale renewable energies, water sanitation

Perez 1983). Furthermore, mainstream STI institutions have historically struggled to recognize 'other' modes of knowledge including indigenous knowledge and community-based knowledge and technologies, although more recently this has arguably shifted to include more decentralized modes as well as more open forms of innovation (Chesbrough, Vanhaverbeke, and West 2006; Hess 2007).

Given these different approaches, and the fact that both are dynamic and develop over time, encounters between grassroots innovations and mainstream STI institutions might imply a negotiation of different meanings and frames of inclusion in the creation of models of inclusive innovation.

Frames and models of inclusive innovation can be regarded as two different – and recursively connected – aspects of the process of building alternative pathways of innovation. According to Snow et al. (1986), framing involves a process of meaning production that allows GIMs to identify and organize their experience in forms that help them to challenge more powerful narratives. In this way, 'collective action frames are action-oriented sets of belief and meanings that inspire and legitimate the activities and campaigns of a social movement organization' (Bendford and Snow 2000, 614). In the case of GIMs, following Jamison (2001), we argue that an important aspect to their framing has been critique of existing mainstream STI and the construction of alternative pathways of innovation and social inclusion. In a recent review article, Smith, Fressoli, and Thomas (2014) identified three broad framings of inclusion and knowledge production in GIMs: *grassroots ingenuity*, emphasizing grassroots knowledge and products catering to the needs of their communities, and which are not provisioned through existing markets and state processes; *grassroots empowerment*, concerning the prospects for transforming local situations, framing innovation as empowering the grassroots to have great control over their futures; and *structural transformation*, which lays emphasis on raising awareness about structural impediments to alternative pathways of innovation, e.g. from mainstream regimes of production and industrial elites.

However, even when frames inform alternative visions, action-repertoires and pathways of innovation, they do not necessarily constitute a blueprint for mobilization and socio-technical experimentation. In order to organize and multiply social actions in a fashion that is readable by mainstream STI institutions, GIMs need to translate their framings into models, and those models in turn have to be legible and meaningful to framings associated with mainstream STI institutions.

Designing models of innovation for inclusion and development implies that there exist ways to formalize, abstract and define variables or principles; and that it is possible to establish logical processes to develop effective and inclusive innovations (and thus policies can be designed following such models).[1] Thus, this tendency of models to be built towards a single or simplified heuristic suggests a challenge for designing and negotiating models of innovation that support GIMs in identifying specific solvable problems, identifying stakeholders, proposing possible modes of participation and knowledge production, and seeking sources of funding.

Ideally, the implementation of a model can also test ideas drawn from different frames and allow processes of learning that would eventually create feedback and transform the framings as well. However, the design and implementation of models is a tricky process. For instance, models can not only be pursued as a means to an end (e.g. fostering a process of participation as part of the innovation process), but also models might come to be regarded as ends in themselves (see Sennet 2008). The latter generally occurs when a technological intervention is regarded as a universal, technological fix for social problems (Schön 1983; Weinberg 1991). This is sometimes attractive to policy-makers and practitioners, though as we shall see, such reductionism may not fit well with the diverse realities and framings of grassroots innovation.

So, behind the abstraction of models, there is usually a negotiation and compromise between different actors over resources, aims and frames of inclusion. How combinations of these different frames are translated into models of innovation, and how those models are subsequently applied, will depend on the political strength and creative capacity of GIMs to negotiate with policy-makers and mainstream institutions.

Some research has tried to characterize how encounters between GIMs and mainstream institutions can lead to the construction of alternative pathways of innovation and development (Hess 2007; Smith 2006). Following these authors, we acknowledge that encounters can be shaped by at least two modes of engagement.

First, there is *insertion* of GIM models of alternative innovation (or at least some of its elements) into wider mainstream policies of STI. The *insertion* mode of institutional engagement proposes to read grassroots creative capacities in ways that make it legible and useful for existing innovation systems and product markets. From the point of view of GIMs, insertion means fitting into prior spaces of innovation and playing by or adapting to the rules of dominant institutions, technologies, regulations, etc. The reverse side of the same movement may happen at the locus of top-down engagement, where mainstream institutions seek to insert and capture ideas, elements and even models from GIMs, adapting them to their own agendas and practices.

Either moving from grassroots up to policy, or from policy down to grassroots, encounters may generate some kind of adjustment and transformation of aims and strategies, leading in some cases to processes of negotiation and construction of models; or they may also lead to appropriation of ideas and products without necessarily being models for alternative pathways of inclusion and development (see Hess 2007; Smith 2006).

If this occurs, giving way to policy disagreements, or if mainstream STI institutions are impenetrable to GIM proposals, a second mode of engagement can arise. This happens when there is *mobilization* or resistance of grassroots to incumbent regimes, with the aim of developing pathways towards alternative innovation systems. In this way, mobilization implies direct attempts to transform the spaces of innovation by challenging the dominant practices, technologies, power relations and discourses. Though mobilization is not a model of grassroots innovation, this perspective is important since it may eventually force the incumbent regimes to change *their* models, and/or lead to autonomous experimentation with new socio-technical arrangements.

Thus, as GIMs interact with mainstream STI agendas, negotiating their models of innovation to enact change (either through engagement or opposition), they face the challenge of having their goals captured and integrated and/or realizing the need to resist and mobilize in order to transform mainstream systems of innovation and technological change. These dynamics are shaped by the interplay of many different influences, such as policy framework and policy culture, the level of community organization, forms of resistance to an imposed technological conformity and the innovators' capacity to generate interest among policy-makers.

In this context, choosing between strategies of insertion and mobilization is necessarily related with the capacities of GIMs, as well as their framings, and the conditions of incumbent STI institutions. As we discuss below in Section 3, all three cases show different strategies of insertion and mobilization in order to build pathways of inclusion; but the context and resistances they face are different, and thus outcomes are very different. In Section 4, we argue that the outcome of these encounters has implications for the construction of models for inclusive innovation.

3. Three GIMs

India and Brazil are currently the sites for notable and internationally visible attempts at developing grassroots innovation. Since the early 2000s, the Social Technologies movement in Brazil has involved activists, public companies and communities seeking innovation agendas and arenas that develop solutions to the problems of those on the margins of economic growth, or who suffer the negative consequences of mainstream growth patterns. In India, the HBN has a 20+ year history, while the PSM offers a longer historical trajectory, originating in the 1980s and with even earlier roots. All three cases presented here indicate attempts to engage with mainstream regimes of innovation and development.

In this section, using documentary analysis from archive material, semi-structured interviews and participant observation,[2] we study how GIMs encounter mainstream STI institutions and what modes of engagement they apply. Hopefully, the analysis of these cases will provide some clues on who and what is being included in innovation models, and under what circumstances, in order that the challenges, limitations and possibilities posed for development can be debated.

3.1. *Honey Bee Network*[3]

The HBN emerged in 1989 among a group of scientists, farmers, academics and others interested in documenting and disseminating traditional knowledge and local innovation in local languages. They focused on ensuring that the individual innovators would receive benefits from their local ingenuity. This was born in part as a response to the Green Revolution of the 1960s and its associated challenges, such as further marginalization of small-scale farmers.

The HBN – an informal network that acts as an umbrella for various others – takes a very precise position on the meaning of 'grassroots innovation': as invention and innovation coming from the grassroots, often among people with little formal training and reliant on local, traditional or indigenous knowledge (HBN 2013). The network's main activity is the scouting and documentation of innovations and traditional knowledge based on different actions such as visiting communities, interviews, awards and competitions. A second step is related to the exploration of the commercial potential of products and processes identified during scouting. This involves not only supporting local grassroots innovators in the process of patenting, but also offering further assistance in terms of prototyping, incubation and seed funding in order to assure commercial viability (Sone 2012).

As just described, the HBN aims to foster creativity and recognition of the capabilities of people to develop their own solutions through their interaction with other innovators, entrepreneurs and supporting governmental institutions. Thus, we characterize its initial framing of knowledge production as a mixture between grassroots ingenuity and grassroots empowerment.

With regard to the engagement of the HBN with mainstream institutions, in its early stages this was intentionally limited, as to a large extent a 'no external funding' principle was adopted over the periods of establishment of the Network in the late 1980s, and its related organizations, SRISTI (established in 1993) and GIAN (established in 1997).[4] Relying on material and non-material contributions from innovators and volunteers, the networks built a strong, values-led mobilized group of members that ensured their sustainability through the 1990s. One of the key mobilization elements are the *shodhyatras* – journeys on foot for up to 15 days to explore the grassroots innovation in villages in different parts of India. This and similar activities have allowed the HBN to connect formal institutions with traditional knowledge holders, making it possible to map around 100,000 ideas, forms of traditional knowledge and innovations.

The sheer amount of ideas surveyed does not allow support for every project or innovation. But almost 200 innovations were given awards by the National Innovation Foundation (NIF), an autonomous institution of the Department of Science and Technology (DST), between 2001 and 2005. In addition, NIF and GIAN have filled patents for 405 innovations. One emblematic success story of the NIF model is the Mitticool fridge, constructed out of clay and working without electricity on the principle of evaporative cooling. After a number of years of experimental activity related to his traditional clay crafts, the inventor – Mansukhbhai Prajapati from Gujarat – benefitted from GIAN's support in product development until he launched the Mitticool fridge in 2005. He was awarded a National Award in its Fifth National Competition for Grassroots Innovations and Traditional Knowledge in 2009. The invention was granted Indian patent No. 240633 and is currently on sale (NIF 2013).

The mode of engagement of the HBN could be described as mainly based on a strategy of mobilization and cautious insertion. As the HBN and associated institutions gained in reputation over the years, encounters with mainstream STI policies have increased. The HBN benefited from the fact that several governmental and non-government bodies were already engaged with similar initiatives of innovation activity based on traditional knowledge in India. Initial support for the work of the HBN from mainstream policy came when the NIF was established in 2000 to strengthen grassroots technological innovations and outstanding traditional knowledge, with Dr R A Mashelkar, former Director General of the Council of Scientific and Industrial Research (CSIR) as its chair. In 1999, the Indian Finance Minister had announced the need to set up a Micro Venture Innovation Fund for helping small innovators and traditional knowledge holders, and in October 2003 the fund was established, with a corpus of Rs. 5 crore (approximately US$1.1 million) (NIF 2004). There have been subsequent changes in the NIF's funding regime, described here only in part. In February 2007, it was announced that NIF would be given the status of an autonomous institution under the DST, with an annual budget of Rs. 8–10 crore per year (approximately US$1.8–2.2 million) (NIF 2007). NIF has also had Memoranda of Understanding with CSIR and Indian Council of Medical Research (ICMR) under which support has been provided to add value to local knowledge (NIF 2010). In June 2010, the pattern of funding was changed from the 'corpus fund' to a regular annual budget. NIF was converted to a grant-in-aid institution under the DST, with a total project outlay of approximately US$5.6 million during the Eleventh Five Year Plan (2007–2012) (NIF 2011).

Thus, based on their previous mobilization, the insertion approach has been successful in facilitating further expansion of the HBN networks – already very broad prior to the initiation of the NIF. They have since spread yet wider to link NIF's work to state-level and national-level governments, banks, firms, research laboratories and civil society organizations. These and the huge networks of volunteers across the country perform the bulk of the work, supported by the staff of around 40.

The NIF was founded in the HBN philosophy, but retains a degree of separation as an autonomous institution within the Indian government's DST, working to scout, document and develop commercial innovations in rural areas of India in order to benefit the masses in India and elsewhere (with a proposal for a global network drawing on the Honey Bee philosophy) (Gupta 2012). This cautious strategy of insertion was only possible due to the political capital generated over many years of the movement's development. Thus, by mobilizing supporters and collaborators widely, HBN retained influence over insertion into policy models.

3.2. *Social Technologies Network*

Originating in Brazil in the early 2000s and suspended in 2012, the STN involved a range of participants, from academics to activists, unions, government representatives, funding agencies and, especially, non-governmental organizations (NGOs) and community groups. Most of these institutions, including several national ministries such as the Ministry of Science and Technology and semi-public companies such as Petrobras, can be considered mainstream STI institutions. So, from early on, the STN was in fact a mixture of grassroots and mainstream STI.

The STN had as its main aim fostering a more democratic process of innovation for development by turning isolated initiatives into broader public policies and application (Miranda, Lopez, and Couto Soares 2011). Those involved with the STN conceived innovation as a tool or catalyst for local development with particular emphasis on empowerment as part of the goal of the interaction between communities and technology developers (Fressoli, Smith, and Thomas 2011). A key goal for the Brazilian STN was building a more socially just relationship between technologists and local communities. To meet this goal, the community must have control over both the process of innovation and the distribution of outcomes. Local groups might not directly be the innovators, but developers make sure that they are fully included in adopting and benefiting from the technology. In other cases, the technology was deliberately developed by local groups, selected by the STN and then scaled up (or reapplied) in engagements between developers and the community in manufacture, maintenance and operation. Thus, the question of empowerment (more than ingenuity) was from the beginning the key frame for inclusion by the STN. Although, in the long term, some actors of the network also saw participation in a local ingenuity frame in developing knowledge solutions as a possible pathway to further social transformation (see Smith, Fressoli, and Thomas 2014).

From 2001, the Banco do Brasil Foundation organized an annual award for Social Technology initiatives (which serves as an invitation to a certification process). An associated database includes hundreds of examples of grassroots innovation, mainly in the areas of agro-ecological production, water recollection and sanitation, education and renewable energy. But only a few of these examples have been selected for reapplication and scaling up, in this way being granted access to funding and support from mainstream STI institutions.

An illustrative example of an encounter between the STN and the state is the One Million Cisterns Programme (P1MC).[5] P1MC, as it became widely known, aimed to build a massive number of water cisterns in a large semi-arid region in Northeast Brazil with a population of around 25 million. The region is characterized by low rainfall and scarce groundwater sources. The family-scale cisterns captured and stored seasonal rainfall sufficient for personal and productive needs (e.g. agriculture) through the drought season.

The cistern programme was originally devised by the Semi-Arid Association, a network of more than 700 institutions, social movements, NGOs and farmers' groups, which later became an important actor of the STN. The Brazilian Ministry of Environment was also initially involved, although the programme was later embraced by the Ministry of Social Development. The Semi-Arid Association itself has its origins in the popular mobilization against dominant paternalistic schemes of aid in the region, known as the 'industry of drought' (indústria da seca). Instead of relying on water supplied by water tanks provided by local political patrons, the Semi-Arid Association proposed to build simple cement-layered containers that collect rainwater from the roof, with a capacity of around 16,000 litres, enough to sustain a family's needs through the region's drought season.

With the arrival of the centre-left government of Lula da Silva in 2003, the Semi-Arid Association found space to insert this programme into national development policies to be funded by the Ministry of Social Development. Later, in 2005, the Cistern Programme also became part of the reapplied technologies of the STN. Since its start in 2003, over 549,000 water cisterns were built and put in place by local inhabitants with the support of the STN and the Ministry of Social Development (MSD 2013). The main feature of the technology is that it is built by its 'users' (farmers/masons, a common archetype of Brazilian semi-arid areas). The self-building aspect of the cisterns is intended to foster relationship-building in the community, through the process of learning to build, use and modify the technology, indicating a grassroots empowerment framing. The water system empowers local people in the building process while also providing autonomy from local governments and water suppliers.

However, the insertion of this model into a government programme became problematic in 2011, when the Brazilian government announced a plan to speed up the implementation of the programme through the purchase of 300,000 plastic water cisterns at almost twice the price of the original cement scheme. Focused on outcomes, this policy change disregarded the process of participation and empowerment that was central to the design of the programme. Also, some private companies saw a business opportunity in the proposal (Dias 2012). Furthermore, early attempts to introduce the plastic cisterns showed design problems, as the plastic cisterns bent and folded due to the intense heat of the region.

The modification of the model by a part of the government (in particular, the Ministry of Integration) provoked a campaign of actions against the plastic cistern initiative, including public meetings and a public rally of 10,000 farmers in the city of Petrolina, in Pernambuco (see Carta Maior, December 20, 2011). Protestors claimed that changes in management excluded and disempowered people. Another element of the controversy included concern that introduction of the plastic cisterns would enable the local political elites to regain power over controlling water, by controlling the distribution and marketing of water cisterns. By the time this attempt of modification of the model had occurred, however, the seed of empowerment had already been planted: banners that waved at the rally contained phrases such as 'We do not want water at any price. We want to participate'. While the government's approach was built around the plastic cistern artefact and the accomplishment of policy goals, the users' approach was mostly concerned with the process and the inclusive dynamics it generated. The capture of the model by the Ministry of Integration led to a controversy about the different technologies that was ultimately a clash of frames about social inclusion.[6]

For almost a decade, the insertion of the model was very successful in building more than 500,000 cisterns and empowering the population of the semi-arid region. However, as a part of the government attempted to strip the programme of its empowerment element and focus instead on inclusion as an outcome, the mobilizations by the movement pushed the Ministry of Social Development to reinstate the self-build cistern programme, though the Ministry of Integration also continued to install some plastic cisterns (Semi-Arid Association 2013). The cistern example shows how the Semi-Arid Association and the STN managed to draw power from mobilization first, to insert their model into the national public policy agenda, and then to resist its capture and modification. Overall, the case shows how the translation of framings of inclusion into models of innovation is not a straightforward process, and how an exclusively instrumental approach to models can oversimplify inclusion against the more complex framings proposed by GIMs.

3.3. *People's Science Movements*

The PSM began in India in the early 1980s, encompassing a range of grassroots networks, organizations and associations, each of which varied in size, history, focus and strategy. The roots of some organizations and networks can be traced back decades earlier. All shared a concern for leveraging a better relationship between science and social needs (Varma 2001). Some of these groups focused on promoting and popularizing science, including through local language education initiatives, to 'reduce disparities in scientific knowledge', while others were more concerned with 'promoting an alternative development model, based on local Indian science and technology' (Varma 2001, 4796).

The PSM grassroots innovation approach came out of discussions in the late 1970s between individuals in national S&T institutions[7] and PSM organizations. These discussions centred on the potential for upgrading traditional techniques through the application of 'modern' science, with particular attention to the achievements and limitations of existing appropriate technology programmes. The PSM approach subsequently differed from prior approaches applied at the CSIR. The latter focused on downsizing modern techniques to make them appropriate for tiny/ micro/small and medium enterprises typical in rural India. The PSM model also differed from the *grassroots ingenuity* approach used at the Khadi and Village Industries Commission, which focused on the upsizing of traditional techniques to modernize the *individual* producer for competition, for example, in the market sectors of leather tanning and product making (Abrol 2012, 2013a).

Instead of focusing on technology development per se, the PSM grassroots innovation approach sought to enable artisans, workers and peasants to function as interlinked *social carriers* of technologiesto organize themselves cooperatively and acquire capabilities for industrial and technological upgrading of local production as 'systems in themselves'. An important feature of the model has been the *open participation of the potential social carriers* in the assessment of technology implementation needs. The PSM grassroots innovation approach has thus included aspects of participatory development of technologies, enhancement of 'user capability' and application of heuristics of 'pro-poor' business models (Abrol 2013a). Further, the PSM approach is embedded in a systemic understanding of the local rural and peri-urban economies, recognizing that (a) all these occupations are interlinked and should be suitably upgraded as a system in order to enhance their collective competitiveness, and (b) when upgraded they should be able to serve the local rural markets and also meet needs of the urban poor not yet addressed by the modern industrial sector (Abrol 2013a).

While being focused on the systems-wide upgrading of traditional knowledge and techniques, the PSM grassroots innovation approach has sought to involve the institutions of mainstream STI in the improvement and commercialization of traditional techniques, and the harnessing of technical improvements in the systems of local production, by building on grassroots ingenuity (indicating an empowering framing). However, like the STN, the PSMs exhibited a dual focus; both on enabling concrete outcomes for marginalized people in India, but also consciousness about the structural barriers to deeper change. The PSMs consequently judge progress jointly to include building capabilities for technology development and implementation *as well as* towards the larger purpose of structural change (Abrol 2013a). In this sense, the PSMs are part of a wider democratic movement motivated by a larger framing of 'structural transformation'.

An emblematic success of the PSMs was around the development of successful group enterprises and broader sectors in cleaner vegetable-based techniques for leather processes. This initiative involved people in tanning, carcass processing and flaying, and more. The vegetable-based tanning technology itself was originally developed in the 1950s by the Central Leather Research Institute, but remained filed on a shelf, unimplemented in practice. The PSMs drew on their knowledge of local economies, framed as area-based production networks, and instead of focusing on the technology artefact, developed a systemic approach, forging an unprecedented collaboration between tanners and flayers (including transcending divisions of caste), developing cooperative enterprises and improving local supplier relationships (Abrol 2013a).

In terms of engagement with mainstream institutions, the PSM in India has based its strategy on both mobilization and cooperation with other social movements in order to better influence and transform mainstream schemes. It thereby achieved the insertion of its own model into S&T institutions. Thus, from an early collaboration with the DST, the PSM was able to insert its model to include schemes across India such as the S&T Application for Weaker Sections, S&T Application for Rural Development, Tribal Sub-Plan, Special Component Plan for Scheduled Castes and S&T for Women and Young Scientists Programme. All these schemes draw on the various characteristics of the PSM approach: a multi-sectoral approach focused on local markets, capabilities and resources; equitable linkages with S&T institutions; and participation of beneficiary groups in all stages of the innovation process.

Furthermore, from their original interventions in the rural non-farm sector, in the mid-1990s, the PSM initiatives have also become active in the farm sector and more recently PSM initiatives have been extended to the implementation of agro-ecological approaches in rural development.

Nevertheless, even after three decades of successful insertion into mainstream STI institutions, the PSM still faces the challenge of how to translate its framing of empowering and structural transformation into readable models.

For instance, the enormous diversity of perspectives, approaches, capabilities, areas of strength, technologies developed for rural areas, and even methods of utilizing DST's support grants, has been a strength as well as a limitation. While the DST suggests that the PSM approach to grassroots innovation should be treated as a general purpose model for funding rural innovation by government agencies in India (DST 2008), there is debate within the PSM about how to retain the original PSM aims towards structural transformation, and how to absorb and nourish the area-specific processes needed for implementing rural innovation across diverse situations (Abrol 2013a).

As a result, new strategies are being experimented to deal with this challenge; for example, the need to link the work on rural non-farm sectors with the implementation of agro-ecological approaches to deal with the challenge of sustainable diffusion of the upgraded systems of local economy in the face of increasing international competition.

4. Discussion

As interest in models of innovation and social inclusion grows among aid agencies and STI institutions, encounters between GIMs and mainstream STI institutions are coming to the fore. However, as we have seen, there are different ways to first, frame both the purposes and forms of inclusion, and second, translate them into models of innovation, with consequences for which elements of an innovation activity become incorporated into models and which get excluded. In this section, based on our analysis of the three cases, we want to highlight three aspects of STI–GIM encounters that may help advance understandings about the contributions and possible limitations of GIMs towards the construction of alternative models of innovation.

The first characteristic is that GIMs should be regarded as active agents open to interaction with mainstream STI agendas, and able to negotiate with mainstream institutions to enact change (either through engagement or opposition). Furthermore, in the encounters, all three GIM networks have used strategies of insertion and mobilization dynamically according to the level of openness and risks of capture that mainstream STI institutions have shown. In the case of HBN, for example, mobilization carefully cultivated legitimacy and cemented grassroots values in order that they might be retained in subsequent insertion into policy support. In the case of STN, as the Cistern model was inserted into a revised policy programme which translated inclusion as an outcome, it prompted mobilization in order to reassert an empowerment framing. Finally, the PSM negotiated a complex combination of popular mobilization and policy insertion from the outset, and while a more rounded model for rural development resulted, the depth of its implementation (or not) remains controversial.

The capacity of GIMs to switch from mobilization to insertion and vice versa, or even combinations, may be regarded not only as a response to the context, but also as a deliberate attempt to retain autonomy. This ability shows that models are not exclusive to mainstream STI institutions, and thus, that social movements are also agents with certain types of power and capacity to make instrumental use of models, as tools to shield their activities and nurture mobilization and alternative ways of knowledge production (Smith and Raven 2012).

The second characteristic is that GIMs have a capacity for reflexive learning, building on lessons gained from previous approaches. Thus, framings seem to arise from a critique on previous initiatives and visions of innovation for inclusion and development (e.g. as a response to appropriate technologies in the case of STN, as a reaction to ignorance about indigenous knowledge in the case of HBN, or to technology-centred approaches in the PSM). By reflecting on the shortcomings of previous approaches and building their unique framings, GIMs can provide powerful alternative pathways of innovation, social inclusion and development to those of incumbent STI institutions.

However, while recognizing this ability of GIMs, it is also important to acknowledge that there are some differences in the ways GIMs have framed grassroots innovation and, by implication, how they approach issues of inclusion. Therefore, although the three cases show some elements of ingenuity, empowerment and structural transformation, they place significant differences in their emphasis. In this way, the HBN emphasizes grassroots ingenuity by putting forward a model for identifying and helping (individual) innovators to pilot and commercialize their innovation. Meanwhile, the STN hinged on a mixture of empowerment and ingenuity with a model based upon development activists co-producing specific innovation objects with local communities who participated fully in the process and outcomes (though STN also developed elements of structural transformation in their framing). Finally, from the beginning, the PSM initiatives have emphasized structural transformation in combination with ideas of empowerment and ingenuity. In this way, PSM seems to have arrived at a more systemic model in which innovations form part of activities for more inclusive economic organization and co-operation in regional clusters. Although more research is needed on the analysis of these differences, it is interesting to note that while ingenuity and empowerment are widely promoted by GIMs and fairly accepted by mainstream STI, the more far-reaching frame of structural transformation proposed by the PSM and the STN still faces difficulties in its translation into models.

The extension of the critique of incumbent models of innovation and the limits of their contribution in attempting to incorporate GIMs is the third characteristic that we want to highlight. Even as grassroots, innovation initiatives are of interest to policy-makers as a means to reach below the radar and bring communities into view, this does not necessarily mean that they will alter broader innovation agendas, institutions and practices. Since mainstream STI can be constrained by its own trajectories and approaches, building new models of innovation and development can be a challenge in terms of resources, extent, aims or space for experimentation, all of which can result in difficult dilemmas for GIMs (Smith, Fressoli, and Thomas 2014). More inclusive models may empower a wider variety of participants to undertake innovation within a particular field, such as energy, but this is not necessarily the same as them having the power to shape the priority agendas for innovation in that field (something influenced by the political economy of STI, and requiring changes in those political and economic relations).

In addition, whereas grassroots initiatives seek context-sensitive solutions, policy pressures to scale up lead to de-contextualized models whose abstractions risk losing sight of the generative situations and alienate those who were involved (such as inattention to local power relations, in the case of the Cistern programme, and the fear by communities of goals being subsumed by political patronage). Indeed, decisions about how to represent groups for inclusion in alternative models, and which representations to include – decisions taken by those with more powerful influence over innovation processes – can effectively disempower and exclude some grassroots perspectives. Inevitably, not everything can be included in the participatory design, prototyping and innovation development; something will be overlooked or communicated poorly in the process, to return disruptively in, say, mobilizations against the exclusions of implementation and commercialization (Asaro 2000). Thus, even when GIMs have a strong mobilized base and good insertion in the STI agenda, the sheer diversity of grassroots experimentation in terms of initiatives, technologies and demands, and the complexity of their framings – which may include elements of empowerment combined with claims for structural transformation – will probably overwhelm the capacity or the willingness of mainstream institutions to accommodate alternative pathways of innovation.

Ultimately, these three aspects of GIM–STI encounters point to a more complex challenge for the construction of models of innovation and social inclusion. This is the challenge of diversity in terms of problems and solutions, claims of empowerment and the heterogeneous layers of demands that GIMs can pose to mainstream STI. In the face of this complexity, it can be very tempting to policy-makers, mainstream STI institutions and even to practitioners in grassroots groups to reduce the diversity of grassroots experimentation to an abstract model that may be measured by simple outcomes. However, a fixed heuristic will overlook the broader framings of GIMs. Regarding models as an end in itself puts pressure on the success or failure of the implementation process, undermining any learning process that might develop. Furthermore, devising models of innovation and social inclusion, as an end in itself, might help to solve emergency situations or provide basic services but hardly will attend to ideas and ways of cultivating deeper forms of grassroots innovation. This seems to be the case regarding the reframing of the model (and of its main goal from empowerment to inclusion as an outcome) suffered by the Semi-Arid Association and the former STN in Brazil. But, as the longer history of the Indian cases shows, not every strategy of insertion is bound to be captured by mainstream STI.

So, if instead of regarding a model as a silver bullet solution, modelling and reflection becomes an element among other strategies of engagement and pathway construction, then more plural means to broader goals and visions of social development and structural transformation could be retained. Seen as part of a pathway, models can be re-conceived as part of processes that constitute spaces of experimentation for different approaches, networks and socio-technical arrangements. But, this perspective requires stakeholders and policy-makers to become appreciative of the complexity of framings, and the difficulties and resistances that they face in the translation into models. The latter option might call for policies to be put into context, and to be honest about the wider power and framings of relations that shape their operation.

5. Conclusions

Models are a necessary step in building pathways to alternative knowledge production and sustainable development. But they are also subject to tensions between different framings of inclusion (i.e. outcomes vs. process) from networks/movements, politicians, funding agencies and stakeholders. The three case study encounters described earlier show a combination of framings (ingenuity/empowerment/transformation) and modes of engagement (insertion/mobilization). We discussed the challenges of retaining control over framings and how they materialize in support for innovation, the risks of capture, and the complexities of representation.

The renewed concern with models of inclusive innovation seems to be a propitious moment for GIMs to propose models and ideas in order to get funding and support. However, negotiations between different framings and practices are not always easy and encounters with mainstream institutions can lead to tensions, controversies or may vary over time. GIMs are active agents in the development of framings and models of innovation for development that can pragmatically use different strategies of engagement in order to negotiate their design and implementation. But at the same time, we acknowledge that strategies vary and take a long time to develop, and movements constantly face setbacks and tensions between their frames and the need to negotiate models. Thus, we argue that it is important to regard models not as a definitive solution to inclusive innovation or as simple instrumental tools for development, but as devices for opening spaces and processes of experimentation, empowerment and alternative ways of knowledge production. This perspective requires stakeholders and policy-makers to become aware of difficulties and resistance that models of inclusive innovation face. Furthermore, this approach requires that processes are provided for reflecting on the operations of the model in practice, and for voicing dissent and revealing power relations, so that the model reveals different framings rather than excluding some. In summary, talk of models needs to avoid discussing them as arrangements for best practice or devices for scaling-up.

Based on the analysis of the cases of the HBN, STN and PSM, this paper suggests that it is important to be attentive to process-based approaches and not only outcome-based models. Thus, it is better to talk about plural spaces for grassroots encounters and engagements in innovation; spaces that are decentred, and provide context-rich experiments in practising technological democracy, as much as they are testing grounds for novel goods and services. While ongoing research will involve deeper exploration of these three empirical cases, our analysis thus far suggests that cultivating spaces for engagement and empowerment is an important policy goal, where the constantly contested and emergent forms of inclusion/exclusion can be explored and new forms of innovation practice can be developed in parallel across different sites and at different scales.

Acknowledgement

We are grateful to the Economic and Social Research Council, whose funding for the STEPS Centre enabled our research into grassroots innovation movements.

Notes

1. Models sometimes emerge to fit what is more easily measureable, i.e. existing statistical data, such as R&D data, while the task of developing models that reflect and respond to more complex realities may be in tension with efforts towards standardization (Arond and Bell 2010; Letty, Shezi, and Mudhara 2012).
2. More information about the methods used in the project can be found at http://steps-centre.org/methods/pathways-methods/cases/historical-contexts/
3. This section draws on a draft paper by Abrol (2013b).
4. SRISTI is the Society for Research and Initiatives for Sustainable Technology and Institutions; the GIAN is the Grassroots Innovations Augmentation Network.
5. The cistern is a simple-layered cement rain water collector designed to be built by the local community.
6. For a description of the different positions in the controversy, see Portal Eco-Debate (2013).
7. These discussions involved Dr Upendra Trivedi of India's DST and Prof. P. N. Chowdury, head of the Centre for Management and Development in the Council of Scientific and Industrial Research. Dr Trivedi was also involved with the National Committee on Science and Technology for the formulation of India's first S&T plan.

References

Abrol, Dinesh. 2012. "Innovations at Grassroots in India: A Historical and Comparative Perspective." Paper presented at STEPS Centre, University of Sussex, Brighton, UK, May 24.

Abrol, Dinesh. 2013a. "Policy Makers and PSMs in the Making of Grassroots Innovation Movements: Indian Experience." Unpublished draft paper. Jawaharlal Nehru University.

Abrol, Dinesh. 2013b. "'Grassroots Innovation' Model, Honey Bee Network and Policy Making." Unpublished draft paper. Jawaharlal Nehru University.

Arond, Elisa, and Martin Bell. 2010. "Trends in the Global Distribution of R&D Since the 1970s: Data, their Interpretation and Limitations." STEPS Working Paper 39, Brighton: STEPS Centre.

Asaro, Peter. 2000. "Transforming Society by Transforming Technology: The Science and Politics of Participatory Design." *Accounting, Management and Information Technologies* 10 (4): 257–290.

Bendford, Robert D., and David A. Snow. 2000. "Framing Process and Social Movements. An Overview and Assessment." *Annual Review of Sociology* 26: 611–639.

Bound, K., and I. Thornton. 2012. "Our Frugal Future: Lessons from India's Innovation System." London, National Endowment for Science, Technology and the Arts. Accessed November 10, 2013. http://www.nesta.org.uk/publications/our-frugal-future-lessons-india%C2%92s-innovation-system

Chesbrough, H., W. Vanhaverbeke, and J. West, eds. 2006. *Open Innovation: Researching a New Paradigm*. Oxford: Oxford Press University.

Cozzens, Susan, and Judith Sutz. 2012. *Innovation in Informal Settings: A Research Agenda*. Ottawa: IDRC.

Dias, Rafael. 2012. "Uma Análise Sociotécnica do Programa Um Milhão de Cisternas (P1MC)." Paper presented at the IX ESOCITE – Latin American Congress of Social Studies of Science and Technology, Mexico City, June 8.

DST (Department of Science and Technology, Government of India). 2008. "Science, Technology and Innovation Policy 2013." http://www.dst.gov.in/sti-policy-eng.pdf

Ely, Adrian, Adrian Smith, Melissa Leach, Ian Scoones, and Andy Stirling. 2013. "Innovation Politics Post Rio+20: Hybrid Pathways to Sustainability?" *Environment and Planning C: Government and Policy* 31 (6): 1063–1081.

Freeman, Chris. 1992. *The Economics of Hope*. London: Pinter.

Fressoli, Mariano, Adrian Smith, and Hernán Thomas. 2011. "From Appropriate to Social Technologies: Some Enduring Dilemmas in Grassroots Innovation Movements for Socially Just Futures". Paper presented at Globelics2011, Buenos Aires, November 15–17.

Gupta, Anil K. 2012. "Innovation, Investment, Enterprise: Generating Sustainable Livelihood at Grassroots through Honey Bee Philosophy." IIMA Working Paper No. 2012-06-04, June 2012.

Gupta, Anil K. 2013. "Tapping the Entrepreneurial Potential of Grassroots Innovation." *Stanford Social Innovation Review*, Special Supplement on Innovation for a Complex World, Summer 2013, pp. 18–20.

HBN (Honey Bee Network) website. 2013. Accessed December 5, 2013. www.sristi.org/hbnew.

Hess, David. 2007. *Alternative Pathways in Science and Industry. Activism, Innovation and the Environment in an Era of Globalization*. Cambridge, MA: MIT Press.

Jamison, Andrew. 2001. *The Making of Green Knowledge: Environmental Politics and Cultural Transformation*. Cambridge: Cambridge University Press.

Letty, B., Z. Shezi, and M. Mudhara. 2012. "An Exploration of Agricultural Grassroots Innovation in South Africa and Implications for Innovation Indicator Development." UNU-MERIT Working Paper 23.

de Mello, L., and M. A. Dutz, eds. 2012. *Promoting Inclusive Growth: Challenges and Policies*. OECD Publishing. http://dx.doi.org/10.1787/9789264168305-en

Miranda, Isabelle, Michelle Lopez, and María Clara CoutoSoares. 2011. "Social Technology Network: Paths for Sustainability." *Innovation and Development* 1 (1): 151–152.

MSD website (Ministry of Social Development). 2013. Accessed April 16, 2013. http://www.mds.gov.br/segurancaalimentar/acessoaagua/cisternas.

NIF website (National Innovation Foundation). 2004. Annual Report 2003–4. Accessed January 25, 2014. http://www.nif.org.in/dwn_files/annual_report/AR0304.pdf.

NIF website (National Innovation Foundation). 2007. Annual Report 2006–7. Accessed January 25, 2014. http://www.nif.org.in/dwn_files/annual_report/Annual-report-2006-07.pdf.

NIF website (National Innovation Foundation). 2010. Annual Report 2009–2010. Accessed January 15, 2014. http://www.nif.org.in/dwn_files/NIF%20ANNUAL%20REPORT%202009-2010.pdf.

NIF website (National Innovation Foundation). 2011. Annual Report 2010–2011. Accessed January 25, 2014. http://www.nif.org.in/dwn_files/NIF%20ANNUAL%20REPORT%202010-11%20English.pdf.

NIF website (National Innovation Foundation). 2013. Accessed December 20, 2013. http://www.nif.org.in/bd/product-detail/mitticool-refrigerator.

OECD (Organisation for Economic Cooperation and Development). 2012a. Innovation for Development: A Discussion of the Issues and an Overview of the Work of the OECD Directorate for Science, Technology and Industry. Paris: Organisation for Economic Cooperation and Development.

OECD (Organisation for Economic Cooperation and Development). 2012b. Innovation and Inclusive Development: Conference Discussion Report, Cape Town, South Africa, 21 November 2012. Paris: Organisation for Economic Cooperation and Development.

Perez, Carlota C. 1983. "Structural Change and Assimilation of New Technologies in the Economic and Social Systems." *Futures* 15 (4): 357–375.

Portal Eco-Debate. 2013. "No Semiárido, Cisternas de Cimento ou Cisternas de Plástico Dividem Opiniões." Accessed December 20. www.ecodebate.com.br.

Prahalad, C. K. 2005. *The Fortune at the Bottom of the Pyramid: Eradicating Poverty through Profits*. Upper Saddle River, NJ: Wharton School Publishing.

Schön, Donald A. 1983. *The Reflective Practitioner. How Professionals Think in Action.* New York: Basic Books.

Semi-Arid Association website. 2013. Accessed June 6, 2013. http://www.asabrasil.org.br/.

Sennet, Richard. 2008. *The Craftsman.* London: Penguin Books.

Smith, A. 2005. "The Alternative Technology Movement: An Analysis of its Framing and Negotiation of Technology Development." *Human Ecology Review Special Issue on Nature Science and Social Movements* 12 (2): 106–119.

Smith, Adrian. 2006. "Green Niches in Sustainable Development: The Case of Organic Food in the United Kingdom." *Environment and Planning C: Government and Policy* 24 (3): 439–458.

Smith, Adrian. 2007. "Translating Sustainabilities between Green Niches and Socio-Technical Regimes." *Technology Analysis & Strategic Management* 19 (4): 427–450.

Smith, Adrian, Mariano Fressoli, and Hernan Thomas. 2014. "Grassroots Innovation Movements: Challenges and Contributions." *Journal of Cleaner Production* 63: 114–124.

Smith, Adrian, and Rob Raven. 2012. "What is Protective Space? Reconsidering Niches in Transitions to Sustainability." *Research Policy* 41 (6): 1025–1036.

Snow, David A., E. Burke Rochford Jr., Steven K. Worden, and Robert D. Bendford. 1986. "Frame Aligment Process, Micromobilization, and Movement Participation." *American Sociological Review* 51 (4): 464–481.

Sone, Lina. 2012. "Innovative Initiatives Supporting Inclusive Innovation in India: Social Business Incubation and Micro Venture Capital." *Technological Forecasting & Social Change* 79 (4): 638–647.

UNDP (United Nations Development Programme). 2010. *Brokering Inclusive Business Models.* New York United Nations Development Programme Private Sector Division.

UNDP (United Nations Development Programme). 2013. Growing Inclusive Markets database. Accessed April 13, 2013. http://cases.growinginclusivemarkets.org/.

Utz, A., and C. Dahlman. 2007. "Promoting Inclusive Innovation in India." In *Unleashing India's Innovation: Towards Sustainable and Inclusive Growth*, edited by A. Utz, 105–128. Washington, DC: World Bank.

Varma, R. 2001. "People's Science Movements and Science Wars?" *Economic and Political Weekly* 36 (52): 4796–4802.

Weinberg, Alvin. 1991. "Can Technology Replace Social Engineering." In *Controlling Technology. Contemporary Issues*, edited by E. B. Thompson, 131–141. Buffalo: Prometheus Books.

Index

Page numbers in *italics* represent figures
Page numbers in **bold** represent tables
Page numbers followed by 'n' refer to notes

INDEX

For Product Safety Concerns and Information please contact our EU
representative GPSR@taylorandfrancis.com Taylor & Francis Verlag GmbH,
Kaufingerstraße 24, 80331 München, Germany

Printed and bound by CPI Group (UK) Ltd, Croydon, CR0 4YY

08/05/2025

01864347-0006